INSIDE OUT

# INSIDE OUT

MY STORY OF BETRAYAL AND COWARDICE

AT THE HEART OF NEW LABOUR

## PETER WATT

WITH ISABEL OAKESHOTT

First published in Great Bri
Biteback Publishing Ltd
Heal House
375 Kennington Lane
London
SE11 5QY

ISBN 978-1-84954-038-4 (cased)
ISBN 978-1-84954-041-4 (limp)

10 9 8 7 6 5 4 3 2 1

A CIP catalogue record for this book is available from the British Library.

Set in Minion and Trade Gothic by Biteback Publishing
Printed and bound in Great Britain by
TJ International Ltd, Padstow, Cornwall

# CONTENTS

# ACKNOWLEDGEMENTS

For years I pursued a career in politics, culminating in becoming General Secretary of the Labour Party in November 2005. I could not have achieved this without sacrificing a huge amount of family life – which is a poor way of saying that I was very often a rubbish father to my children and husband to my wife. So let me up front thank my wife Vilma and children Ben, Ivanna, Anya, Gabriella and Ruby for still seeing me as a fundamentally decent husband and dad despite the fact that I so often failed to put them first.

I was lucky that my parents, Sandra and David, were such great role models and they, together with my large and diverse group of nine brothers and sisters, have been, and continue to be, an inspiration and incredible source of strength. My children are lucky to belong to such a wonderful extended family.

There are so many people at the Labour Party I should thank that to name any would be to risk forgetting some. Over the years I have met, worked with and been inspired by an incredible number of people in the party, many whom will never have their contributions recognised publicly. The party has been lucky to have such a talented and dedicated group working for it. I'd like to single out Roy and Alicia Kennedy, Hilary Perrin and Marianna Trian as being some of the best friends I could have hoped for. Over the years we made a formidable team.

Producing this book was not easy but my ghost writer Isabel made it easier. I hope that I was a good fellow author – I know that she was great. Thanks also to Iain Dale and the Biteback team.

When I resigned as General Secretary of the party in November 2007 I was devastated. At times I thought that the pressure of the situation, the humiliation I felt and the pain of perceived betrayal would consume me. The fact that they didn't, that I came through them and in many ways am stronger for them, is down to Vilma. She kept me sane, told me when I was wallowing in self-pity, protected me when necessary and stood by me. For that, which I am not sure I deserve, I am eternally grateful.

*Peter Watt*

This book has been a labour of love, the work squeezed into late nights and weekends when I should have been spending time with my husband and son. It distracted me from deep sadness during a painful period in our lives, and helped keep the darkness at bay. I would like to thank Nigel for his endless indulgence, wise counsel and patience as I threw myself into Peter's story. I owe Rollo an apology for spending so much time on the computer – it is lucky that toddlers are so forgiving. I would also like to thank Editha Briere, a wonderful person without whom it would probably have been an impossible mission, and my parents and sisters for their endless support. I am also grateful to Paul Richards, former Labour special adviser, and Humfrey Hunter, our agent, who was brave to take on a political book in a difficult financial climate. He dealt with the unexpected challenges professionally and cheerfully. I would also like to thank Charles Hymas of the *Sunday Times* for his encouragement. I dedicate this book to Nigel and Rollo.

*Isabel Oakeshott*

*December 2009*

# PREFACE

BY ISABEL OAKESHOTT

I first met Peter Watt the day after the Crown Prosecution Service announced he would not face charges, in May 2009.

A mutual friend had put us in touch during his long wait for a decision and I would phone him now and again to see if there was any news.

More than a year went by with no word on Peter's case.

Though I didn't know him, I felt sorry for him being stuck in this seemingly endless limbo and made occasional calls to the CPS in the vain hope that media interest might chivvy them along.

Whenever we spoke, Peter always promised to give me his first big interview if he was cleared, and he was as good as his word. I called him as soon as the CPS made its announcement and the following day we met at the City Inn at Westminster, where he poured his heart out about the way he had been treated by the Labour leadership.

He seemed more hurt than angry or embittered. I had not delved into the rights and wrongs of the case, but he clearly felt he had been deeply wronged by Labour's high command and wanted to set the record straight.

He had so much to say that there and then, I floated the idea of working on a book together. I had been looking for a big project and it was obvious that I could not possibly do his story justice with one interview in the *Sunday Times*.

Peter seemed open to the idea, and over the long parliamentary summer recess we met a couple of times to discuss how it might work. I was quietly testing whether he had enough interesting material to make the project a success and I suspect he was quietly working out whether he really wanted to do it.

He would give me political insights gleaned from his friends in the Labour Party which sometimes worked as immediate stories for the *Sunday Times*, while I would sound him out about various subjects relating to his time as General Secretary.

I was dismayed that he had not kept a personal diary while in office, but it quickly transpired that he had a highly unusual memory for detail. He was a colour writer's dream, offering up a stream of entertaining anecdotes and vivid description without much prompting. He also had many interesting revelations about one of the most tumultuous periods of the Blair/Brown years.

I am not a big fan of heavy political books, and it was the sense that Peter had a compelling human interest story as well as serious information that appealed to me. He spoke very movingly about the death of his father, his marriage and his role as a foster parent, and was very open about his feelings. He was funny and self-deprecating, and I warmed to him immensely.

We began working on the book seriously in August, writing against the clock to complete it by Christmas in time for publication before the general election. We both felt that there was public interest in the book being published. However, in the event that there was a change of government in 2010, the significance of the Blair/Brown era would diminish amid the excitement of a new administration. Neither of us wanted to write a book that felt like ancient history.

Naturally Peter was wary about the timing. He remains a member of the Labour Party and a party donor. He still firmly believes that Labour offers the best solutions to the challenges facing this country. By writing this book, and publishing before the election, he knows he will face a backlash from some in the party, who will accuse him of disloyalty.

But as he says, loyalty is a two-way street. After reading about his experiences, perhaps those critics will understand why blind loyalty is no longer something he is willing or able to give.

This is his story.

# 1. EXIT

On 27 November 2007, I resigned as General Secretary of the Labour Party in one of the biggest political scandals of the Labour administration. As I left our headquarters via a back door I was in an almost trance-like state. I was embroiled in a crisis over donations which was threatening to engulf the party leadership and would soon escalate into a criminal investigation.

I slipped out of Labour HQ without public tears or fanfare, my jacket and belongings discreetly scooped up by my loyal chief of staff, Marianna Trian. After a day of high drama, nobody wanted another scene. On the surface, I was just about holding it together. But inside I was falling apart.

As I made my way to the platforms at Waterloo station my BlackBerry buzzed incessantly, the vibrations zigzagging through my head. My nerves were taut as drum skin. I moved silently across the station concourse, sweat pricking my underarms.

Then I saw myself on a huge television screen by the departures board, my face grotesquely magnified. My whole nightmare situation danced above me in awful high definition and I imagined a thousand pairs of eyes swivelling my way. I hurried along the platform, head bowed like a salesman trying to get away after a dishonest deal. I remember wondering if I was going insane.

Mechanically, I boarded the 9.10 p.m. to Poole, heading for the sanctuary of my family. It was only when I finally sat down that I began checking my voicemails. There was one from Jack Straw.

'Peter, it's Jack,' he said. 'I can't talk right now. But whatever you do, *don't resign*. I might be able to help.'

But it was too late.

It had all begun so differently, with champagne, balloons and hearty handshakes. When I was appointed General Secretary, cards and warm wishes poured in, Tony Blair rang me personally to offer his congratulations, and it seemed like everybody wanted to be my friend. The title came with a £100,000 salary, invitations to private dinners with the Prime Minister, and automatic entry to the corridors of power. I spent my days with powerful people, dealt with multi-million-pound budgets, rubbed shoulders with billionaires, and had half of Downing Street on speed dial. The ultimate backroom boy, I knew where the bodies were buried, and did what I could to keep the show on the road.

As you can imagine, all this made me feel pretty important. Thanks to my job, I was at the heart of some of the most sensitive dealings of the party in government; a vital link between Tony Blair and Gordon Brown when relations were frayed, and a keeper of many interesting secrets. Before long I began to feel quite invincible.

Landing the job was the culmination of more than a decade of unglamorous hard graft, and a commitment to the party stretching back to my teenage years. I was incredibly proud of it, never more so than when, a few months before everything went pear shaped, Mum and Dad were invited to Downing Street to meet Tony shortly before he left office. As soon as he sauntered into the room where my parents and I were waiting, he started teasing me. Until that moment, when they saw the Prime Minister of the country joshing with their son, I don't think Mum and Dad fully realised what my job meant.

Day to day, I was in charge of 1,001 things, and it was incredibly demanding on every level.

A 'perk' of the job was attending political Cabinet meetings, which took place around once a month, immediately after the normal government Cabinet session. The civil servants would withdraw and myself and other political staff like Philip Gould would go in. For an hour or so there would be a discussion on the latest political situation led by the Prime Minister. The first time I attended I was very excited – this was after all the Cabinet of Her Majesty's Government and I was sitting at the table. I didn't stay excited for long. The discussions were long and turgid and ministers would not always bother listening to each other. I would look round the table and see people doodling or gazing vacantly into thin air. Occasionally contributions were top quality but generally the calibre of debate was very poor indeed.

Often my job would collide with normal family life in the most surreal ways. A phone call I took six days after I got the job in November 2005 set the tone. It was a Sunday and my wife Vilma and I were at my parents' house in Poole. We had just popped out to pick up some milk from the newsagent. As we crossed the street, I tripped over my shoelaces and went sprawling onto my arse, right in the middle of the road. At that exact moment, my mobile rang with the Prime Minister on the line. I was struggling to get up from the tarmac, cars swerving around me, trying to sound brisk and efficient as he asked me if I could prepare some report for the next day.

Some of the issues I dealt with had incredibly high stakes, threatening the very survival of the government, but behind the scenes at Labour Party headquarters on Victoria Street in London, we often had a good laugh.

John Prescott's affair with Tracey Temple provided great sport. We were in the middle of a difficult local election campaign when news of the relationship broke. I was as amazed as everyone else to discover John's secret, but on a personal level I was worried about him. I was very fond of him, and knew him to be a proud man, so I knew he must be going through hell.

On the day news of the affair broke in the press, he rang me to apologise. Though he had no need to, he's an honourable man and I think he thought he should speak to the party in some official way about what had happened. As I was the General Secretary that meant me.

'Hi Peter, obviously you've seen the story,' he said.

'Yeah, it must be awful for you. Are you okay?' I asked.

'It's terrible timing for the party, right in the middle of the election campaign. I feel so responsible,' he replied miserably.

'Look, John, these things happen. It will be okay,' I said, trying to make him feel better.

We didn't talk long, and I tried to be supportive – I knew it must be a dreadful time for him and his wife Pauline.

As we were in the middle of a local election campaign, we were having daily early morning meetings – usually attended by myself; Ian McCartney, party chair; Philip Gould, Tony Blair's pollster; JP (John Prescott); Ben Wegg-Prosser, director of No. 10's Strategic Communications Unit; John McTernan, Blair's political secretary; Spencer Livermore, Gordon Brown's director of political strategy; Alicia Kennedy, Deputy General Secretary; and Marianna.

After the story broke, there was such a media scrum around JP wherever he went that he became a virtual prisoner at Westminster and could no longer attend. I didn't expect to see him at all that week, but on the Thursday, I received a phone call from Joan Hammell, his special adviser, to say he was going to come to the meeting the next day.

Those Friday meetings were often cancelled, with people finding various excuses for not turning up. However, when word got out that JP was coming, I could have sold tickets for the event. The entire No. 10 team arrived, plus Spencer from No. 11 – unheard of for a Friday morning – and loads of other hangers-on. They all crowded into the room, and we tried to get all the bad taste jokes out of the way before JP arrived. We couldn't wait to see his sheepish expression when he walked into the room. But as we were all sitting there waiting for the big arrival, I got a phone call from Joan Hammell, JP's special adviser, to say he couldn't make it after all. As soon as they heard, most of the No. 10 lot just left – they didn't even bother pretending they'd come to talk about the campaign.

Poor JP: none of the details of his fling with Tracey were pretty, but the worst was a story about the size of his manhood that had appeared in *The Sun*. It was illustrated with a half-page picture of a chipolata sausage. Some joker in the office had cut it out and stuck it on the wall behind my desk, just above head level if you were sitting down. I hadn't noticed.

The following Monday, Joan rang again, to say JP wanted to come into HQ to see me. He wanted to touch base and catch up on how the campaign was going. I was doing some paperwork as I waited for him to arrive, and looked up to see him heading towards me across our open plan office. For some reason I swivelled slightly in my chair. It was only then, with JP a few paces away, that I saw the picture of the sausage.

As subtly as I could, trying to keep a neutral expression, I pulled it off the wall and shoved it under my desk. I came within an inch of having a conversation with the Deputy Prime Minister, with a picture of a chipolata representing his penis right behind my head.

So there had been some great comedy moments, but by late autumn 2007, I was feeling pretty low. Ever since Vilma and I got married, I had been working incredibly long hours. I was even taking work calls on our wedding day on New Year's Eve 2003. At the time I had another demanding post in the party and was very focused on climbing the career ladder. Looking back, I can't believe my attitude. I'm sure the Labour Party would not have ceased to function if I'd turned my phone off for the day. I suppose I thought I was so important I should always be on call.

Once I became General Secretary, it just never stopped. I would start taking calls at around 8 a.m., and my phone would not stop ringing till at least eleven every night. It could be anyone on the line, from a senior trade union official to the Prime Minister himself, who once called me at 4 a.m. just for an update on something.

As you can imagine, all this was very intrusive on family life. My job took over everything, and I simply never switched off. Vilma and I had a chaotic house full of children, some our own, others fostered, and it was an incredible strain trying to be a big shot at the office as well as Superdad.

It didn't matter where we went – if someone wanted to get hold of me, they would track me down. One weekend we went to stay with my brother Damien and his wife Janice at their lovely place in rural Dorset. There is very little mobile reception in the village of Morden and the only spot where you could get a signal at Damien's house was at the top of a little hillock in the garden.

I'd had a horrendous week at work – we were in the middle of yet another crisis – and I had spent the entire 2½-hour journey down on the phone, poor Vilma trying to drive and keep all hell from breaking loose in the back of the car as the kids grew restless.

When we arrived, my brother and I disappeared to the local pub, a few miles away, for a quiet drink. There was no point taking my phone, because there was no signal at the pub either. It was a classic snug country place, with a crackling fire and cosy seats, and after a couple of pints, I was just beginning to relax. Suddenly, the man behind the bar came rushing out, saying he'd had a phone call on the pub landline from Damien's house – we were needed urgently back home.

Damien said he would go and he drove like a bat out of hell through the country lanes, thinking something dreadful had happened to one of the kids, only to find it was just JP. He'd told Vilma he needed to speak to me and that it was important, and she took him at his word. It turned out he wanted advice on what to say on the BBC's *Politics Show* the next day. Damien returned to the pub with a mobile phone that he knew would work and I spent half an hour sitting by the fire drinking my pint and talking to JP, sotto voce because it wasn't exactly a Labour-supporting area. I have no idea how he tracked me down to Damien's place, but it just went to show I could never escape.

It was partly my own fault. My job was about building alliances and allegiances, keeping the different factions of the party happy. To do it properly, you really had to be accessible to everyone, from senior politicians to the NEC,* the trade unionists and party staff. My view was that if one of my staff felt they needed to phone me out of hours, it was important to them; therefore I had to deal with it. So I didn't actively discourage these out-of-hours calls. The truth is, they nearly killed my marriage.

I don't know how Vilma put up with it for so long. I was always someone else's property, and it must have been really difficult for her. She couldn't plan anything without ringing my office, because I didn't know what had been scheduled for me. Sometimes, the party even dictated what I wore. For keynote speeches or important appearances, I might be

---

* The National Executive Committee is the party's equivalent of a board of directors. It is made up of sections, with thirteen members from the trade unions, six from local Labour parties, and the remainder made up of MPs, MEPs, local councillors, members of the government, a black and ethnic minority representative plus the leader and deputy leader of the party. Most people are elected by their section to serve two-year terms. The General Secretary is an ex-officio member.

The NEC is responsible for the party's staffing, finances, rule book, annual conference and election preparation. In reality many of its functions are delegated to senior staff or its sub-committees. It meets every other month. In between meetings the small sub-group of NEC officers meets to take decisions and hear reports as required.

asked to put on a certain tie to fit in with the colour scheme of the stage set, and if Vilma hated the tie – well, that was too bad. While I prided myself on being wonderfully empathetic to colleagues and emotionally intelligent about work problems, I was not nearly as sensitive at home.

When I was feeling good about the direction of the party, I could justify in my own mind the ridiculous hours I was working. But by autumn 2007, just before my spectacular exit from the job, I was no longer feeling good. There had been a tremendous high in the Labour Party when Gordon took over from Tony that summer. For an all-too-brief period, it seemed as though we had pulled off the supposedly impossible – a trouble-free transfer of power from one Prime Minister to another – and were riding high in the polls. Winning a fourth term suddenly seemed a realistic dream.

But by November the political landscape looked totally different. Our huge poll lead over the Tories had evaporated and we were languishing 11 points behind David Cameron in the polls. Thanks to some serious cock-ups and misjudgements, it seemed we had thrown it all away. Every day brought new tribulations, and I was struggling to motivate myself, never mind the staff.

I was troubled by my relationship with Harriet Harman, which was becoming strained. She wanted staff, not an unreasonable request, since she had just become deputy leader. The problem was that we had no spare staff and no spare money to employ anyone additional. I seconded someone to her team on a temporary basis but she wasn't happy. Our relationship became more tense when she suggested I ask the NEC to change the rules so that there would always be a woman as either leader or deputy leader. I said I thought this would be a mistake and after consulting colleagues, including Mike Griffiths (chair of the NEC at the time), who shared my view, I refused. The problem was exacerbated by the fact that No. 10 was not sure how to involve her in decision making and as a consequence she felt that she was being kept out of the loop.

Meanwhile Downing Street was a total shambles: there was no vision, no strategy, no co-ordination. It was completely dysfunctional. Gordon had been so desperate to become Prime Minister, and had plotted so meticulously and ruthlessly to get to No. 10, that we all assumed he knew what he was going to do when he got there. Perhaps naively, I imagined that there was some grand plan, tucked away in a drawer, that he, Ed Balls and the rest of the crew had been working on for months, or even years. It's not as if they hadn't had ages to work out what they actually hoped to achieve once they got their feet under the table. However, if any such document existed, nobody seemed to know about it. I think they all assumed someone else had written it. Gordon was simply making it up as he went along.

There were mutterings across Whitehall about what a mess No. 10 was in. Decisions about the most trivial things would take weeks, because nobody felt confident enough to sign anything off themselves. Everything was referred up to the next level in a tortuous process which did not stop until it reached the top. Only then, if you were lucky, would you finally get a response.

At party HQ we couldn't get answers to the simplest of questions – even getting the okay to send out an anodyne email to members took an age. Imagine what it was like for civil servants, trying to get Downing Street to sign off major political decisions! It had become clear that the machinery of No. 10 was simply not up to the job.

Things were so dire that Murray Elder and I were planning to go and see Gordon and raise our concerns. Murray was one of Gordon's oldest and most trusted friends, one of just a handful of people he confided in and listened to. They had been at school together in Scotland. It was a relationship that Murray handled very discreetly, greatly to his credit. Everyone knew he had Gordon's ear, and he was often used as a conduit to raise delicate issues.

He and I had built up a rapport over the years, as he had had a minor role in fundraising when I was the party's finance director. Throughout 2006 and the first half of 2007, we also met very regularly to discuss plans for the leadership transition. It was all very low key – Gordon would want to know about the work that was going on at HQ to prepare for his takeover from Tony, and I would give Murray assurances that we were making preparations.

As time went by, Murray and I also began talking in more detail about how well prepared Gordon was for becoming Prime Minister. Our conversations were always very positive and constructive. If Gordon had some worry about whether we were doing the groundwork for the takeover, it was usually Murray I'd hear it from.

Murray and I continued having these regular chats after Gordon became leader, usually at a quiet corner table in the Elgin Room in the House of Lords. While we sat there, me drinking coffee, Murray sipping water, Labour peers such as Swraj Paul, Kumar Bhattacharyya and other important figures would often stop by for a quiet word about their own concerns over the way Gordon was handling things.

We had reached the point where we felt we needed to sit down with Gordon privately, and see if we could persuade him to sharpen up the No. 10 machine. Murray undertook to email Gordon, and a date was fixed for the three of us to get together a few days later. This was a big step for Murray, and the fact he agreed to it showed just how serious and widespread the concern was within the party and Whitehall about the state of things at Downing Street. Neither of us was looking forward to explaining this to the Prime Minister.

To make matters worse, Vilma had finally had enough of playing second fiddle to my work. In October 2007, she gave me an ultimatum – it was her or my job. Until that moment, I don't think I'd fully understood how unhappy she was. I could see she was deadly serious. I had six months to sort myself out.

It was against this miserable backdrop that the scandal which was to end my career unfolded – and I never made the meeting with Murray and Gordon. However, plenty of interesting things happened before my dramatic exit.

## 2. AGAINST THE ODDS

My career with the Labour Party began almost as dramatically as it ended. I did not win the job of General Secretary without a bitter fight.

I was not Tony's choice for the position, a misfortune that should have ended my chances. However, it was a position I desperately wanted and, defying advice from colleagues, I'd decided to campaign for it anyway.

Wise friends at work warned me I would lose everything if I picked this fight with No. 10. After all, I would be asking senior party figures to vote against what the Prime Minister wanted – not a great career move. If I failed to pull it off, there would be no way back. 'You're mad,' they said, urging me to content myself with the job I had.

But I was bloody minded and though I knew it was crazy, the position was a big prize and I was prepared to risk everything to get it.

My kamikaze mission began in autumn 2005, after Matt Carter, then General Secretary, announced his resignation from the post.

Unusually, that summer, he had taken the whole of August off, and had been completely uncontactable by phone or email. As the most senior party official around in his absence, I had been running the show, and I loved it. Matt returned in September, very relaxed and distant, and it was obvious something was up. He asked his PA, Vic Gould, to set up a phone line in one of the meeting rooms and block-booked it for twenty-four hours, hanging a 'Do Not Disturb' sign on the door. He kept disappearing inside for long periods, and we all assumed he was talking to Downing Street about leaving his job.

The next day he took me into the boardroom, and told me privately that he planned to quit. He had spent the summer talking it over with his family, he said, and had decided it was time to move on. He looked very at ease with what must have been a huge decision, as if a weight was off his shoulders.

'I hope you'll consider applying for the job. I think you'd make a very good General Secretary,' he said.

I tried not to show my excitement. 'Thanks. I'll think about it,' I said casually, but I knew straight away that I would.

I went outside for a cigarette and fell into conversation with a fellow smoker, a junior colleague called Sarah.

'Is Matt going?' she asked.

'I don't know,' I pretended, because it was not yet official, but she knew I knew.

'I really hope you are going to go for it,' she said.

Within an hour of my meeting with Matt, lots of people were urging me to stand. I was very excited, and became quite carried away imagining myself in the post. In my own mind, it was a done deal. I made a beeline for Marianna and Alicia Kennedy to tell them my news.

'I'm going for the job,' I blurted. I was so caught up in my fantasy it hadn't even occurred to me that Alicia might want to run for the position herself. She was senior to me, and I certainly should have discussed it with her first, something I regret.

That night, I talked to Vilma, pretending I was still thinking it over, and wanted her input. It was an out-and-out lie, and she wasn't taken in. She played along for about five minutes before levelling with me. 'I don't know why you are even asking what I think, because it's obvious you've already made up your mind,' she said.

Though she was right, I did want to warn her about the pressure and strain the job could put on our family. 'You need to be absolutely sure about this, because our lives really will be turned upside down,' I said.

'I know,' she replied – but in truth she had no idea what was in store and neither did I.

Matt's resignation was formally announced in a press release, and a timetable for the election of his successor was agreed with the NEC officers. His leaving date was 31 December, and his replacement would be selected at the NEC's annual awayday at the beginning of November, allowing a few weeks for the handover.

By the end of the week, I began telling people I was going to stand, and was receiving a lot of encouragement. Already I was completely obsessed about it. The power had gone to my head before I was even in the job, and I was almost salivating at the prospect of being in charge.

Though the appointment would officially be decided by a secret ballot of the thirty-two members of the NEC, there was always a backroom deal. Anyone who wanted the job needed the endorsement of the Prime Minister, who always got the candidate he wanted.

I wasn't sure what Tony made of me, especially since I hadn't been particularly deferential the first time we met. It was in 1999 and I was quite a junior figure in the party, working on our elections and membership team. I'd been asked by my then boss, Margaret McDonagh, to go to No. 10 with the head of my team, Carol Linforth, to give a presentation to Tony and JP about the state of party membership. The message from the grassroots was blunt: they thought Tony was doing a good job in government but neglecting the party, and many were not sure about renewing their subscriptions. I didn't mince my words, and I think JP thought I was a jumped-up whippersnapper. Tony sat and listened carefully, smiling at me rather indulgently. I later found out that he did not forget how I'd 'told him off' that day, though he didn't hold it against me.

Whatever his first impression, I was hoping I could dazzle him at party conference. We were anticipating some controversy that year over a strike by British Airways ground workers, who had walked out in sympathy over the treatment of staff working for a BA catering supplier, Gate Gourmet. The issue for the party was whether workers should be allowed to stage secondary (or support) strikes. Tony was vehemently against support strikes, but many people in the party took a different view. Worryingly for No. 10, it was possible that the leadership could be defeated by the NEC on the issue, creating the damaging impression of a party at war with itself. It was going to be a fantastic opportunity to showcase my negotiating skills, and the lengths to which I would go to swing votes in favour of the leadership.

However, I was keenly aware that getting the job was more about securing support from people in the Downing Street political office than Tony himself. He had bigger things to worry about and would be guided by them. The most important figures were John McTernan, Tony's political secretary; Ruth Turner, No. 10's director of government relations, who had Tony's ear; a guy called Razi Rahman, who had a party management role; and Nita Clarke, who looked after trade unions. I also needed some trade unions to throw their weight behind me, and in mid-September I spent a couple of days hobnobbing at the TUC congress in Brighton in an attempt to get two or three of them on side.

I was getting good vibes from everyone and thought I pretty much had it sewn up. I felt that I had more than proven my credentials for the job. I had spent three years working at a senior level in party HQ helping enforce party discipline; I understood party finance; I had often shown my willingness to throw myself in front of bullets for the leadership, and I had played a key part easing controversial proposals from No. 10 through the party's policy-making process. Time and again I had gone above and beyond the call of duty to ensure Tony won difficult votes. For my pains, I was sometimes considered a bête noire by the unions, but I had a good relationship with most of their political officers, and was generally seen as a safe pair of hands. I was also popular with staff and had the backing of the outgoing General Secretary.

However, a few days after the TUC, Matt called me into the boardroom, shutting the door behind him. 'Just to let you know John McTernan's not supporting you for the job,' he said.

My face fell: this was a body blow. John's backing was critical to securing Tony's endorsement. 'Do you know why not?' I asked, shocked.

Matt couldn't shed much light on it, except that John wanted to back someone called Ray Collins, a trade union figure who had high-level Labour Party connections. I asked Matt where Tony stood.

'He's keeping an open mind,' he replied.

Through the grapevine, I discovered that Ray had some very influential personal friends in the party, including Nita and Margaret McDonagh, a former General Secretary of the party. Apparently, Margaret thought I was too young for such a big job, and believed that Ray, who was more experienced, would be easier to work with. Ray had another powerful ally in Margaret Prosser, a former member of the NEC and a former senior figure in the T&G union.

I was absolutely gutted and went out for a smoke to calm my nerves. I found myself confiding in Sarah again. 'I think I'm finished. John's not supporting me, so Tony won't,' I said gloomily.

'Don't be ridiculous!' she scolded. 'It's early days. You can't just give up.'

So I slept on it for twenty-four hours, then decided to ring John myself. 'I know you'll make your decision according to what you think is in the best interests of the Labour Party. All I'd ask is that you don't make up your mind right away. You know I'm a loyalist and I will do whatever Tony wants. If he doesn't want me to run, I won't, but I'm not sure we're at that stage yet,' I said.

John listened respectfully and I felt he took my words on board. I was glad, since whatever happened, we would be working together very closely at conference. Matt had made it clear to me that since he was leaving soon, he was not going to play an active part. He hoped that by stepping back, he would be giving me a good chance to prove I could deliver. I was excited: I enjoyed the political management of difficult issues and I would now be operating at the most senior level.

It turned out to be a very difficult conference, as the issue over workers' rights to stage secondary strikes ignited. The NEC threatened to defy Tony's position, triggering panic in the leadership. Nobody could remember such a thing happening before, and the consequences could have been very serious. Through most delicate negotiation, often dragging on late into the night, John, Ian McCartney and I somehow saved the day, and Tony prevailed. Though I was completely drained, I left Brighton on a high, feeling I'd done an excellent job. I was sure I must have impressed John.

My surge of optimism was short lived, for within a few hours Matt rang saying John was going to back Ray anyway. It felt like a total kick in the teeth and I was furious. I had given it my all at conference, and thought John and I had worked very well together. I couldn't work out why he was so determined to support Ray.

There was one small consolation: Tony had agreed to speak to both of us before he finally made up his mind. We were asked to write a confidential memo setting out our ideas for the future organisation and development of the Labour Party, as a test.

I decided I only had one shot at this and was unlikely to win any points for sitting on the fence, so I proposed radical changes that I knew Tony would like. My memo, written with Matt's help, criticised the power of the handful of trade union barons who controlled party policy and proposed sweeping reforms to our relationship with them. I called on Tony to back more state funding of political parties, knowing that if we reduced the influence of the trade unions, they would reduce their financial support accordingly. I outlined other reforms I knew some in the party would hate, hoping they would chime with the Prime Minister's modernising agenda.

My bid to become General Secretary was now becoming quite stressful, and I was struggling to concentrate on anything else. I was still supposed to be running the party finances, but I was hopelessly distracted. More importantly, I was beginning to sniff danger. I knew that if I pushed too hard, I risked losing everything. On the other hand, it appeared there was still an outside chance I could win Tony's backing, and while this sliver of hope remained, I would not throw in the towel.

I decided to take the following Friday off work to try to restore some sense of perspective, and went down to Poole to see Dad. He was always a wise counsellor in times of crisis and I often resolved things in my head by pouring out my heart to him on a long country walk. We would ramble along the Dorset coastal path for five or six hours, then find a pub and ring Mum to come and pick us up, while we settled down for a meal and a few beers.

We set off at a gentle pace, and I told him what had been going on. We were just having a breather on a hill when John rang to say Tony wanted to see me and Ray the next week to talk about the job. A few minutes later, Razi called for a chat.

What was becoming increasingly clear was that the political office at No. 10 was divided over who should get the post, and the debate was becoming quite personal. Razi and Ruth were supporting me, while John and Nita wanted Ray.

'I think it's good news that Tony wants to see you next week,' Razi said, as I paced around.

It was freezing cold and overcast, and Dad, who was hanging around at a discreet distance, looked like he wanted to get going.

'Hmm,' I replied doubtfully, though I was pleased too.

'He's not just listening to John, he's listening to Ruth as well. There's still all to play for,' Razi added encouragingly.

I knew how seriously Tony listened to Ruth, and began to feel a bit less pessimistic.

I returned to work feeling better. Though Marianna and Alicia were still supportive of my bid, by now they were cautioning me against burning my bridges. However, in my own mind my position was crystallising: I was ready to stake everything.

'If I don't get it I'm going to leave. I've already pushed so hard that I don't think I could work with whoever gets it now, and if I were them, I would not want me around either,' I told them.

They thought I was exaggerating, but I knew it was now winner-take-all, or as I put it crudely, 'fuck or bust'. That Tuesday, I went to see Tony as planned, and we discussed my memo. As I'd hoped, he agreed with my ideas.

'Is there anything else you want to throw in?' he asked at the end.

I was ready for this. 'What I would say to you is that you need a General Secretary who knows how to cover your back when the going gets tough. I'm sure your political skills and powers of persuasion have gone a long way to making sure you have prevailed at conference and at national policy forums, but don't underestimate the extent to which I, and colleagues, have helped that happen behind the scenes. When you make your decision, just make sure you remember that,' I said boldly.

Tony gave a sort of half-smile, amused at my directness. 'Well, that's telling me then, isn't it?' he replied genially.

I left Downing Street feeling I had done as much as I could, passing Ray on his way in to see Tony. Back at HQ, I told Marianna and Alicia what I had said.

'Oh my God, did you really say that to him?' they said, shocked.

'Yeah, fuck or bust,' I grinned. The expression became an in-joke. They began teasing that I was no longer safe to be seen with.

A few days later John called again. 'Tony doesn't want you to stand. He's going to support Ray,' he said bluntly.

I was amazed. 'I've told everyone I'm standing!' I protested. 'You can't ask me not to stand. Stand and be beaten, okay, but not stand at all?'

That night I went to the pub for a colleague's leaving do in a foul mood. I spent the night drinking too much and banging on to anyone who would listen about the injustice of it all. An inebriated conversation with a colleague brought me to my senses.

'Get a grip,' she slurred. 'Why don't you fight for this – run it like a mini election campaign? After all we've done enough of them. Work out who is on your side, and who's backing Ray. Work out how many you've got to win over, and get on with it.'

'Hmm, that's a plan,' I thought, suddenly cheered. It hadn't occurred to me that I could fight on.

Later, I spoke to Ruth, telling her that while I would do what Tony wanted, I was really unhappy that he wasn't even letting me run.

'Let me check that is what he wants,' she said anxiously, suggesting there might have been crossed wires. A little later she rang me back. 'I've arranged for you to see him,' she said. 'He's decided to back Ray, but I don't think he would stop you from standing.'

A couple of days later I made my way over to No. 10 hoping she was right.

'It was a close-run thing, Peter, but as you know, I've decided to back Ray,' Tony confirmed.

'I understand,' I replied evenly. 'What do you want me to do? Do you want me to stand? If you don't, I won't, but you need to understand that if I run, I am going to campaign for the job – I'm not going to put myself up as a patsy.' If I was going to go down, I was going to go down fighting.

'Of course I understand that,' Tony nodded, my green light.

That night I drew up an Excel spreadsheet, listing all the members of the NEC. On the most pessimistic assumption, twenty-nine of them would vote for Ray, and three would vote for me. The most optimistic figures were eighteen for Ray, fourteen for me. It meant I needed to firm up eleven people, and convert another three.

I rang Alicia, slightly hysterical. 'Tony has said I can run. It's fuck or bust,' I declared dramatically.

'You're crazy,' she said seriously. 'Just stop. There is no way you can win this. Think about it.' She stressed how much pressure members of the NEC would be under to vote in favour of Tony's candidate on the day of the ballot.

She was absolutely right, but I was deaf to all reason. I'd already gone too far.

I sat down and worked out a strategy. Paradoxically, my most valuable asset was that I was not Downing Street's official candidate. Plenty of members of the NEC had ideological differences with Tony, and I planned to exploit them to the hilt. There was no point pretending I was not a Blairite moderniser, but I decided to present myself as a General Secretary who would stand up for their interests and would not be intimidated by No. 10. I was ruthless and shameless in my approach: cajoling, flattering, reasoning, pressurising. I would not take no for an answer.

'I know Tony is backing Ray, and I respect that, but I would like you to give me ten minutes of your time, to tell you why I think I would make a good General Secretary,' I would say, and despite all the pressure they were under from No. 10 to fall into line, virtually everyone I approached listened.

By now No. 10 was conducting a powerful operation against me. I had no axe to grind – it was their job to push for the candidate Tony wanted – but it was very unnerving. I would get vaguely menacing messages from Downing Street via third parties, saying that there was an 'instruction from No. 10' that I should stop campaigning. I reminded myself that Tony had said I could do it. However, there was no longer any doubt that if I did not get this job, I would have to clear my desk. It was quite liberating in a way: I no longer had anything to lose.

The situation was very difficult for colleagues at HQ, who found their loyalties divided between me and the party leadership. In a bizarre state of affairs, No. 10 was running an operation supporting Ray, while

I, arguably one of the most powerful figures at HQ, was running an operation against him. The truth was that the party machine at Victoria Street, while not actively supporting me, was not exactly throwing its weight behind my rival. Sometimes I would be in a meeting with one of the NEC representatives asking for their support, and as we talked they would get a call from someone in No. 10, pressing them to back Ray. As for the Treasury, publicly they had no view on the matter, but privately, Gordon's people wanted me to win, purely because I was not Tony's candidate. It was the usual tribalism.

Of particular importance to my bid was Mike Griffiths. Mike was a senior member of the NEC trusted by other members. He was the national political officer from the trade union Amicus. He was also my friend and he personally secured the support of his trade union and lobbied many other members of the NEC on my behalf.

Though Alicia and Marianna still thought I was mad, as the weeks went by the number of people Ray could rely on to back him slowly fell, and I was beginning to enjoy myself. I was already so proud of working for the Labour Party that sometimes I had to pinch myself to be sure it was true. To be General Secretary, the equivalent of chief executive of the organisation, would be the pinnacle of my career. I knew the challenges would be huge: there would be a leadership election when Tony left office (he was not expected to serve a full third term); we had to turn around our decline in the polls following the Iraq War; and there was the prospect of fighting for a fourth term. But what an adrenalin fix! I didn't give any thought to what I would do if I lost.

Poor Vilma was the one who suffered. I remember one evening when the kids were being particularly boisterous and we took them out for tea at a pizza place to stop them bouncing off the walls. I spent all but fifteen minutes on the phone outside the restaurant, while my wife battled to keep the children under control. Looking back, it's bizarre that I didn't realise just how hacked off Vilma was. She does a good line in glowering, but I was so wrapped up in my own importance that if she'd actually had a go at me, I think I'd have accused her of being unreasonable.

The final interview was due to take place at a trade union training centre in Esher. Each candidate was to give a twenty-minute presentation to the whole NEC, followed by questions. In the run-up to the big day, there were apologies from some who couldn't make it. In the end, only twenty-eight were expected to vote, and the numbers shifted in my favour.

I arrived in Esher on the Sunday night feeling surprisingly calm. I thought I looked the part. Once upon a time, I had a pink Mohican – I used to bleach my hair blond before dunking my head in bright-coloured dye. The bleach base layer really made it suck up the colour. I thought it was fantastic. But I had long since grown up and scrubbed up, and was in my best suit for the occasion. I practised my presentation in my bedroom. I had printed it off in large font, highlighting areas for pauses and emphasis to ensure I didn't gabble. Despite my selfish behaviour, Vilma was being very supportive – I think she secretly hoped that whatever happened, I would get my fixation with this job out of my system. She probably realised that if she had tried to stop me doing this, I would have been too self-obsessed to listen. We had a brief chat on the phone that night, and I promised to ring her in the morning so she could wish me a final good luck.

I had figured out that if everyone on the NEC voted the way they had privately pledged, I was two votes ahead of Ray. All the same, I knew they would be under intense pressure from No. 10. Too nervous to eat on the morning of the interview, I rehearsed my presentation a final time in front of the mirror, and had it virtually word perfect. I was buoyed by the news that another of Ray's supporters had been unable to make it.

As I walked into the interview room, Marianna and Alicia glanced at me encouragingly.

'Welcome, Peter,' Jeremy Beecham, the chair, said, gesturing at me to begin.

After weeks of angst and tension over this job, I suddenly felt really confident and relaxed. I was genuinely excited. 'I'm going to sock it to them,' I thought. I opened my mouth to speak – and absolutely nothing came out.

It was a classic case of stage fright, but I was stunned; it had never happened to me before. I opened my mouth and tried again, and all that came out was a funny croak. I physically could not make the muscles function. I shot a look at Marianna and Alicia, and though I could barely focus, I could see they looked worried. Bees buzzed in my head; I began to feel dizzy.

'I'm panicking,' I thought to myself. Everyone looked at me expectantly. As I tried to get a grip, I remember thinking, 'I'm going to lose my job, and it's going to be really humiliating, and I am dying on my feet before I've even started.'

Mechanically, I reached down for the glass of water on the table in front of me, and took two very deliberate sips. It seemed to flick the switch.

'Thank you, Jeremy, and good morning,' I said confidently, just as I had rehearsed. I proceeded to give a virtuoso performance.

I glanced around the room and it occurred to me that my supporters were a real motley crew: a strange coalition of trade unionists, people on the hard left and passionate Blairites.

I fielded the questions which followed my presentation without difficulty, and headed up to my room to await the result.

'This is it,' I thought to myself as I paced around. 'Fuck or bust.'

Alicia texted to say Ray had just finished, and they were about to start voting.

About six minutes later, she sent another text. 'And the winner is. . .' I read, but the message ended there. I grimaced – she was teasing. About thirty seconds later, my phone beeped again. 'You.'

There was a knock at the door. It was Jeremy with his congratulations. The votes were sixteen to me, eleven to Ray: I'd pulled it off by a good margin.

I phoned Vilma. 'I've done it!' I exclaimed, hardly believing it myself. She was thrilled. 'What time are you coming home?' she asked happily.

I stopped short. 'I'm not,' I said slowly, realising I'd failed to make it clear that I'd be away for another night if I won. To my horror, I discovered she'd organised a celebration party with friends and family, and had spent the day making special food. She was really sad, and I was mortified. It was a genuine case of miscommunication, my fault for being too absorbed in my campaign to make my plans clear.

That evening, I made a point of contacting Ian, who was not around because he was unwell. I knew he had wanted Ray, and felt it was important to build bridges immediately. He was full of hearty congratulations on the phone, but I knew he was upset and angry at the way things had turned out. It took several months and a trip to his constituency in Wigan for us to develop a good working relationship.

The other person I was worried about was John. I called Razi, who talked him into coming over to Esher for a few drinks, so that everybody could see there were no hard feelings. We were going to have to work closely together, and I wanted him to know I didn't hold his failure to back me for the job against him. Surprisingly, it was the beginning of a real friendship.

I was expecting a phone call from Tony during dinner that evening. Knowing the mobile signal in the training centre was bad, I had cased out a good spot where I could take his call. At 8 p.m., the Downing Street switchboard rang with the PM on the line.

'Peter!' he said cheerfully.

'Tony!' I replied happily.

'What have you done?' he teased. I could tell by his voice he was smiling.

'Sorry!' I replied, in a jokey voice.

'If you'd told me you were going to campaign that hard and win, I might not have let you run,' he quipped.

I decided to level with him about the extent to which I'd exploited my status as the candidate he did not want. 'Look, you've probably heard I played the No. 10 card to my advantage.'

'Hmm, I have heard,' he replied.

'Well, just to make it absolutely clear, I am *your* General Secretary,' I said.

He had been around the block enough to understand.

Ruth Turner had been listening in to the call. 'He's really pleased, you know. We need to make sure that you and he get together quickly,' she said, after he'd hung up.

Back in Poole, Mum and Dad had been to a Labour meeting. Mum told me she'd walked into the room, and asked everyone if they'd heard the party had a new General Secretary.

'It's my son,' she declared proudly.

The following day, Tony attended a full meeting of the NEC in Esher. He shook my hand ostentatiously and was very warm.

When I arrived back at Victoria Street that afternoon, I felt like I'd been away for a month. As I walked into the office, a huge cheer went up. Matt Carter gave a little speech, and I was ushered off to have my photo taken, which, being vain, I wasn't very happy about, because I looked tired and drawn. Later, I sat down with Marianna, and asked her to be my chief of staff, and Alicia, who agreed to be my deputy. Elated, I headed home.

Vilma had put up 'Congratulations' bunting, and managed to persuade most of the people she'd originally invited for the previous evening to come and welcome me. She really pulled out all the stops, arranging another surprise for me a week later. She was very mysterious about it, liaising with my secretary to book an evening of my time so that we could 'go out for the night together'. The negotiation with the office that this involved was a sober reminder of what I'd let my family in for: from now on, someone else was managing my life. On the night, she led me to a wine bar in Battersea, where she'd booked a function room for a celebration with all our friends from the Labour Party, social services and her family. It was all fantastic, but even then I knew we had embarked on a roller-coaster ride. Looking back at the photos I notice there wasn't a grey hair on my head.

# 3. HOOKED

I remember the exact moment I decided I wanted to work for the Labour Party. I was a nurse specialising in elderly care at Poole Hospital, but I had been dabbling in local politics for a while, and was becoming increasingly intoxicated by this very different, high-octane world. I was standing as a Labour candidate for the local council and had become involved in a national party campaign called Operation Toehold. Even the name gave me a thrill, making me feel like a spy on some covert mission. Its objective was to get at least one Labour councillor on every council in England with no Labour councillors at that time.

One such place was Poole and our preparations for the 1995 local elections were overseen by three exotic visitors from Head Office. Ian McNicol, Naomi Grove and Geoff Dixon were all hard-nosed party organisers and I was enthralled by them. I had never met anyone who was actually paid to work in politics before.

The polls were held on 4 May 1995, and I waited for the count with breathless excitement. Though we failed to win Harbour by fifty-four votes, we did get three Labour councillors onto Poole Council. It was a real breakthrough and we went to the house of two local activists, Ken and Gill Greening, to celebrate and watch the coverage from other parts of the country.

In the early hours of the morning, John Prescott came on TV to talk about the results. He was speaking from Walworth Road, the then national party HQ, and behind him were a group of staffers on the phone. Ian, Naomi and Geoff knew the staff and so Ian used his mobile to call one of them there and then. As JP talked live on TV, Ian was telling his mate to scratch his ear or raise his hand in the background. I watched as his mate did a discreet little jig just for our benefit. I was mesmerised – such power! It confirmed what I had been thinking for some time: I wanted to do this for a living.

Though I was in my late twenties by this time, I'd been interested in politics since I was a child. Dad used to regale us with stories about his time as a Labour candidate in the 1960s for a marginal council seat in York. It was the first time he'd run for election but his agent was an experienced operator. With a week or so to go until polling day, there were more Tory posters up than Labour ones and Dad was feeling despondent. His agent bet him a couple of pints that he could change all that in one evening.

The agent began knocking on the doors of houses with Tory posters and telling the residents that he was from the Conservative Party and that he had to collect in the posters due to a technical problem. They were duly handed over. The poster situation was reversed, Dad bought the man a beer, the Tories complained of dirty tricks, and Dad lost.

I'm not quite sure why I'm repeating the story, apart from the fact that it makes me smile, but it shows that politics was a family affair. From an early age I was aware that Dad was a Labour supporter. His mother always proudly told how in old age she would get the Tories to take her to the polls, where she would duly vote Labour. However, my maternal grandmother was a Tory and was angry that Dad had poisoned Mum's mind with what she regarded as 'socialist filth'. I can remember Dad going off to a party conference in Blackpool in the early 1970s and bringing his mother-in-law back some 'educational material'. I'm not sure that she thought it was as funny as he did.

However it was the Catholic Church, not politics, that was the biggest influence on our family. Our church was St Mary's in Poole, and we all attended St Mary's School. Fr McCaffrey, Fr McGivern, Fr Costello and Fr Bennet, our priests, were all bigger figures in my early life than Jim Callaghan, Denis Healey or Tony Benn. Church was where we went every week and met friends, and the distinction between school, home and church was blurred.

I should stress that my upbringing wasn't fire and brimstone. I didn't grow up terrified of going to hell if I did anything wrong. I had a loving home, went to a caring school and adored going to church. Unlike many children who are coerced into it by their devout parents, I genuinely enjoyed being an altar server and loved the smell of incense. It all gave me a clear sense of valuing other people and the importance of community, family and caring for others less fortunate. I think that even when I turned my back on the church in my teens, a phase that lasted for twenty years, it remained a fundamental part of who I was.

I was born in York on 20 July 1969 – the day that Neil Armstrong landed on the moon. I was the first of my parents David and Sandra's ten children. Their fourth child, my brother David, died just before he was born on 9 November 1974, a tragedy that broke their hearts. In order of birth, the rest of the family are Bernadette (Berni) – 1970, Damien – 1972, Timothy – 1976, Philip – 1978, Gerardine – 1981, Jason – 1981, Amber – 1992, Toby – 2000. Jason, Amber and Toby are all adopted.

My first school was St Anne's in Keighley but when I was four years old Dad got a job as a nursing officer at Poole Hospital in Dorset and we moved. Dad was always busy working long hours, and money was tight as the family was growing, but I was happy. My parents, who married young, began fostering children soon after they were married, and there was always a new child or children staying with us for a few days, weeks or longer. I loved it most of the time and two of the kids, Mevalyn and Valerie, are still close family members to this day.

On the Friday after Labour lost the 1979 general election, when I was nearly ten, I spent my lunch break arguing with Madge, one of the dinner ladies, that Labour would be back soon and that the small size of the Tory majority would undo them. I wasn't the only political commentator to get it wrong that day.

I left St Mary's and went to Poole Grammar School. I remember having a debate with my parents about whether it was politically right for me to attend a grammar. Dad reassured me that he thought it was fine, and though I still felt uncomfortable about it in principle, I was secretly relieved as the school had a good reputation and I was looking forward to enrolling.

It was a good school academically but I didn't enjoy my time there. By the time I was fifteen, I was wearing a CND badge and was organising collections of money and food outside our church for the striking miners. The headmaster, Mr Gilpin, asked me to take off my badge at school, but I wasn't giving it up without a fight. I asked him to explain why other pupils were allowed to wear Army Cadet badges and I couldn't wear my 'symbol of peace'. To his great credit he spent an hour discussing this with me and my friend Lee Fisher in his office. In the end we couldn't agree but he got us to compromise. He promised to establish a political notice board where we could display articles if we took off the badges.

I briefly joined the Young Socialists but the attraction was fleeting. It felt more like a cult than a political party, with membership determined by how many copies of *Militant* you sold. I wouldn't sell any so my membership was short lived. By 1985 I was disillusioned. I felt that the leadership of the National Union of Mineworkers had let down its brave members and played right into Margaret Thatcher's hands. I fretted that the hard left were destroying the Labour Party. I remember bunking off school to watch the TUC and Labour Party conferences. I sat at home with a pretend cold and applauded Neil Kinnock's famous 1985 conference speech when he condemned the Militant Labour-controlled Liverpool Council.

After taking my O-levels I set my heart on becoming a nurse, having seen how much Dad loved the job. It was, and still is, an unusual career choice for a man. My grammar school careers service wanted me to be a doctor and couldn't understand why I was aiming for what they described as second best. I was outraged and my political conscience, by now inflamed by adolescence, kicked in hard. In a fit of pique, I flounced out of school, deciding to do my A-levels at the local college rather than stay a moment longer at this snobby institution.

It was just the start of a long rebellious phase. Free from the social conservatism of the grammar, I really let loose. My girlfriend Claire shaved my hair into a Mohican and I pierced my ears. Dad was horrified – but for him it could only get worse. In the months that followed, I dyed my hair using a variety of bright colours, wore Goth clothes, increased the number of piercings to seven and spent most weekends off my face on booze. Not surprisingly, I wasn't particularly applying myself at college. Things came to a head just after New Year's Eve in 1987, when I walked out of home and college with most of the second year of my A-level course still to go. I crashed at friends and studied my A-levels alone using borrowed course books. I took the exams as an independent student and passed. Why did I do this? Hormones, booze and being a bit of a prat all played their part.

I needed money, so after my A-levels I came to my senses, ditched the Mohican and piercings, and began looking for a job, starting out as a computer operator for Barclays Bank, despite having no clue about computers. I really enjoyed it, and definitely liked the money, but I still wanted to be a nurse and in September 1989 I began a three-year Registered General Nurse course based at the nursing college attached to Poole Hospital. I was the only male student in a class of thirty, and loved the attention. The assumption that I was gay meant that I was soon 'one of the girls'. Vilma thinks that I've always been in touch with my feminine side and she's probably right.

I was enormously proud when I qualified in 1992. My real passion was for geriatric care. It's a specialism that's often looked down on in the medical profession, but I was amazed by the dedication and skill of staff who devoted themselves to this field and it seemed to suit me. Immediately after qualifying I began working in the Philip Arnold Unit in Poole Hospital, a group of about five wards that specialised in care of the elderly. My period working there, firstly on Brownsea Ward and then on Longfleet Ward, was one of the happiest and most satisfying times of my adult life. The work was physically hard and often emotional, but I was very proud to be part of the team.

Though I was very absorbed in my nursing work, I had not forgotten politics. After Labour lost the 1992 general election I felt guilty at my complete lack of personal effort to stop another Tory victory. I don't think I was alone. I decided to join the Labour Party again. It took a while to find out how to do it: Poole isn't exactly traditional Labour territory, and indeed at that point there were no Labour councillors on the local authority at all. I managed to track some Labour activists down, and in late 1992 attended my very first party meeting.

I definitely wasn't inspired. I arrived just before the meeting was supposed to start, at 6.30 p.m., and there wasn't a soul there. By 6.45 there were five of us, but the secretary had not turned up. He finally showed at 7.00, only to announce that for personal reasons he was resigning, and by 7.15 I was secretary of the branch!

Over the next few months I was drawn into the heady world of local politics and I loved it. Poole Labour Party was full of characters, all unique, often larger than life and always committed to the cause, whatever the cause was. One of the people I particularly enjoyed working with at that time was Tony Gardner, who had been MP for Rushcliffe from 1966 to 1970, before losing to Ken Clarke. He was the only man I know who could canvass while smoking and get away with it, and he took me on my first session out on the stump one Sunday morning. He became a very close friend and gave me my first introduction to planning a campaign and writing leaflets. Brian Jones was another doughty campaigner and stalwart; Ken and Gill Greening were trade union activists and kept snakes; and Bob and Mal O'Mahoney ran the Poole party. Along with many others they became personal friends and slowly but surely I became more and more hooked on the political drug.

The problem with addictions of course is that they need bigger and bigger fixes to be satisfied, and more and more of my spare time was being taken up by the Labour Party. I remember trying to run a local by-election campaign while I was at work on Longfleet Ward at the hospital. I was running around with a bright yellow brick-sized mobile phone trying to talk to campaign HQ (someone's house) about leaflets and manage the doctors' ward round at the same time.

As a trainee nurse I had begun a relationship with a colleague called Donna who was an auxiliary nurse. After only a few months we decided to get married, and in 1991 we did just that. She was three months pregnant, and on 7 July 1991 Benjamin was born. It's funny looking back how shocked I was at how disruptive a new-born baby is.

Hindsight is a wonderful thing but I think that we were too young, and I was certainly too selfish, for marriage. It wasn't easy. We tried marriage guidance, but it made little difference: I was still selfish, as the counsellor pointed out. Whenever I wasn't working, I was either out on

Labour Party business or in the hospital social club. I looked after Ben when Donna was at work and when she was at home I was out. In June 1994 Donna told me that she was pregnant again, and Anya was born on 24 January 1995. It was too late, though – our marriage was over, and despite dragging out the formal ending, in autumn 1995 I left and moved back to Parkstone House, the nurses' accommodation hostel at the hospital.

Ironically, a few months earlier Donna and I had moved in with my parents in an attempt to save money for a deposit on a house. Our separation meant me moving out from Mum and Dad's house, leaving Donna, Ben and Anya living with them. The result was that Donna became very close to my parents, almost like another daughter to them.

It was around this time that I became involved in Operation Toehold and decided I wanted to go into politics full time. However, it took me over a year to get anywhere. There weren't many paid jobs for the party and it was a hard grind getting my foot through the door.

Despite Geoff telling me at one point I would make a bloody useless organiser, and failing to get the first eight jobs I went for, in June 1996 I finally got my first break. I was offered the position of local organiser to Battersea Labour Party.

On Saturday 31 August I left Poole, my family, my two children and my job as a nurse and moved to a bedsit just off the Wandsworth Road in a pretty rough part of south London. My parents drove to the city to drop me off and Mum cried when she left – she thought the area was unsafe. On Monday 2 September 1996 I started work for the Labour Party.

# 4. PROJECT CAKE

Soon after I became General Secretary, I started work on a secret project codenamed 'Cake'. This was the name we gave to plans being drawn up for swapping the most electorally successful Labour Prime Minister in our history for Gordon Brown.

Though Tony Blair had publicly declared during the 2005 general election campaign that he would serve 'a full third term', privately he had always made it clear he would give his successor plenty of time to settle in before the next general election. It meant that at some point, we at Labour headquarters were going to have to manage a leadership contest, or, if nobody stood against Gordon, work out how to engineer the transition of power from Tony to the Chancellor within our party rules.

Though we went to great lengths to ensure it never leaked, contingency planning for a leadership election actually began as far back as January 2004, when there was speculation Tony might have to resign. We took it seriously: he was facing a very dangerous period of his premiership, with a potentially disastrous vote on university top-up fees scheduled for the very same day as the publication of the long-awaited and potentially career-ending report by Lord Hutton into the circumstances surrounding the death of Dr David Kelly.

Around 100 Labour backbenchers were threatening to rebel over plans to introduce £3,000-a-year fees for students. There was a real possibility that if Hutton pointed the finger at Tony over Kelly's death, and he was defeated in the Commons on the education bill that same day, his position would become untenable. As Labour's director of compliance, one of the senior roles I held before becoming General Secretary, part of my job was to anticipate problems, and I thought it was a good idea to know what would happen if Tony suddenly quit. Our party rules were not designed to allow for changing leaders between general elections and there were serious obstacles to overcome in our constitution if we were to do this. In fact, the rules, which dated back to the 1980s, were specifically designed to entrench the position of the party leader, to prevent destabilising leadership challenges.

I spent some time mapping out what would happen if Tony suddenly decided he couldn't go on, asking John Sharpe, one of the party's solicitors, to write me a confidential paper about what the rules might mean in those circumstances. I hadn't told Matt Carter about this work, and when John copied Matt in to his advice without warning me, Matt totally freaked out. He was terrified that it would get out, and it would look as if we had written Tony off before Hutton and the vote had even taken place. I argued that we had to make contingency plans and he reluctantly agreed.

The week before the Hutton report and the education vote, Matt, Alicia Kennedy and I held a very confidential meeting. We talked through all the issues that would arise if Tony didn't survive, and tried to ensure we were ready for any questions that came our way.

In the event, he scraped through the education vote by the skin of his teeth, and the Hutton report near enough exonerated the government. Tony survived, and our contingency plans were put under lock and key in a bottom drawer.

I did not return to the leadership subject until I became General Secretary in November 2005. At one of the first meetings I held with my senior team, I told them I believed my time in the post would be judged on two things: how well we managed the transition from Tony to his successor; and the next general election. We agreed to start holding regular meetings – myself, Alicia and Roy Kennedy, Hilary Perrin (who managed our regional offices) and Marianna, to flesh out how the transition would work.

We were totally paranoid about details of these meetings leaking – or even the fact that they were taking place. It was winter 2005, only a few months since Tony had told voters he would be staying put until the next general election, which was not expected to take place until 2010. Imagine what effect it would have had on his premiership if it became known that Labour headquarters was already planning his exit! The Tories would have pounced on the information as evidence that he was already a lame duck, and Gordon Brown's supporters would have interpreted it as a sign that the Chancellor was likely to become Prime Minister sooner than later. It would have been incredibly destabilising.

So we went to great lengths to ensure nobody knew about the meetings except the five of us. We were careful never to leave anything lying around the office that might give the game away, ensuring all paperwork was numbered when it was handed out at the start of a meeting, and counted in at the end. When it was time for the planning meeting, one of us would say to the others 'Let's go and get a coffee and some cake' as a signal to head off to a private room, and so the meetings became known between us as Project Cake.

During this period, I used to meet Tony at least once a month, Gordon about every six weeks, and John Prescott, who as deputy party leader was a pivotal figure in the transition, every fortnight. As Project Cake developed, these meetings became increasingly important. Despite this, for most of the time, Tony, Gordon and JP were only peripherally aware that planning was taking place at Head Office. They certainly didn't know just how much detailed work was being undertaken.

It quickly became clear from these meetings that Tony was in no hurry to leave: he still had important things he still wanted to achieve. It was mainly public sector reform – he felt there was still a very long way to go and wanted to lock in the changes he felt were necessary before Gordon took over. It was clear he did not trust the Chancellor to continue his work. Meanwhile it was evident from my meetings with JP and Gordon that they did not trust Tony to leave office until the last possible moment. JP would say things like 'Gordon just wants to push Tony out, and that's unacceptable and wrong.' On the other hand he sympathised with Gordon. 'I can understand why he feels so frustrated, because Tony won't commit. He keeps saying he'll go, but he won't say when,' he would say.

During this period, I was trying to ride two horses and it was bloody difficult. It was not just about negotiating the details of the transition, but other aspects of my job, which increasingly had to be agreed by the Chancellor and the Prime Minister, who had different agendas.

For example, Tony wanted to make various controversial reforms to the party relating to the trade unions, and was becoming increasingly frustrated at his lack of progress. His objective was to reduce their power. He was uncomfortable about the 'block vote' the unions had on party policy, since the reality was that power was vested in half a dozen trade union general secretaries, rather than the members themselves. Tony felt, and I agreed, that the block vote was a stitch-up masquerading as working-class democracy. However, Gordon kept blocking Tony's attempts to change the system. Understandably, he didn't want to rock the boat with the unions before he became leader, since he would need their support to secure the job. So it was very difficult to get anywhere. I couldn't push any of Tony's proposed reforms forward unless they were rubber-stamped by Gordon. Just because Tony wanted it to happen was no longer enough. If Tony forced the issue then Gordon made it quite clear to me that he wouldn't support the proposals. In effect this would sabotage the plans and Tony would be further weakened.

I told Tony that I wanted to stay in my job after he'd gone. Pissing Gordon off wasn't a great career move and I felt pulled in opposite directions whenever issues such as trade union reform were raised. Increasing numbers of people, whether Cabinet ministers or senior party officials, were beginning to feel the same way.

I was constantly to-ing and fro-ing between the Prime Minister and the Chancellor, trying to keep them both happy. At Labour HQ, it was becoming increasingly difficult to do our jobs effectively, because of the endless negotiation involved between No. 10 and No. 11 on every decision, from relatively minor things like the colour of the stage set for conferences, to more important issues such as the narrative for local elections or the strategy for a by-election. We were beginning to look ridiculous to the wider party, who saw the constant dithering as a sign of our weakness. In the past, Downing Street would agree something, and we would make it happen. Now, we had to go through the tortuous process of ensuring Gordon was signed up to everything, which led to a lot of confusion, delay and buck passing.

The regular meetings with No. 10 and No. 11 often involved discussing aspects of Project Cake. Meetings at the Treasury would typically involve Sue Nye, Spencer Livermore and Jonathan Ashworth; while the No. 10 meetings would be with Ruth and Ben Wegg-Prosser. The meetings had quite a different feel. Those in No. 11 took place in a little room, and we sat round a table quite formally and went through an agenda. Marianna and I would try to work out in advance what would upset Gordon's people, and think of ways to defuse potential flash points. The discussion points were quite broad – for example, we debated whether there should be a three-month transition or a snap transfer of power. Meetings in No. 10 were in Ruth's office, which she shared with Matthew Taylor. He would discreetly disappear while we discussed things in a far more relaxed way than we did in No. 11. I felt more at ease, and the discussions seemed more candid.

Fundamentally, all these meetings were about when and how Tony would go. The rest was window dressing. A major sticking point was whether Tony would remain an MP when he left office. Gordon did not want Tony to stand down as the MP for Sedgefield, fearing that the by-election this would trigger would draw attention away from the early days of his premiership. There was the danger that it would become a referendum on Gordon becoming Prime Minister, and that if Labour lost the constituency it would ruin any political honeymoon. There was also the issue of cost: by-elections are expensive, and we were always struggling for cash. However, Tony was keen to make a clean break. Gordon's team thought he was just being selfish, deliberately making life more difficult for them, but there wasn't much they could do about it.

As 2006 wore on, Gordon became increasingly frustrated with the uncertainty over when Tony was going. The Prime Minister was repeatedly asked in public about his plans but never gave anything away. It made Gordon more and more suspicious that he wouldn't keep his word about stepping down well before the next election. Behind the scenes, it seemed to me that No. 10 was trying hard to extend olive branches to the fractious Chancellor, but he and his entourage seemed unable or unwilling to respond in kind. Often we found that either we did not consult No. 11 enough about decisions, and they sulked; or we consulted them too fully, and they went over the top, throwing their weight around and acting as if Gordon was already leader.

I never ceased to be amazed at the hopeless lack of communication and contact between the Treasury and No. 10 throughout 2006. No. 11 effectively operated like a party within a party, with JP conducting shuttle diplomacy between Gordon and Tony or their people. JP knew I was talking to the Treasury and No. 10 and, on the whole, trusted me. There were times when I became frustrated that one side or the other was digging its heels in on an issue, and JP would step in and bang heads together. As time went on he became increasingly frustrated with both sides. He tried to force the pace, not least because he wanted out himself. He would get really wound up when Tony and Gordon wouldn't agree on something and say things like 'If this issue isn't resolved by next week, then I'm going to go public, and say I've had enough.'

As time went on he became increasingly serious about those threats. But in the end it was Gordon and his supporters who forced Tony's hand. They got what they were after, but I think the ugly way they went about it damaged the Chancellor's prospects of being a success as Prime Minister before he even began.

# 5. CASH BUT NO HONOUR

## A £13 MILLION SECRET

One of the strangest aspects of my time as General Secretary was that for all but a few months I was under police investigation. It's a sorry distinction and I still can't quite believe it. Until I took the job, my closest brush with the law was probably getting a parking ticket. So to find myself caught up in a criminal inquiry while I was working for Labour not once, but twice, was devastating.

Perhaps it shouldn't have come as such a shock, since I had long been worried that the party would one day inadvertently find itself on the wrong side of the law. The reality was that over the years we had been very blasé about our financial and administrative arrangements, and did not take sufficient care to ensure that everything we did was legal. The government had pushed through new laws tightening up the regulation of political party funding and improving data protection, measures we had made quite a song and a dance about. It all dated back to Tony's promise to voters in 1997 that we would be 'whiter than white'. But for some reason, often we forgot that the measures the government passed actually applied to us as well.

We had some pretty close shaves. Soon after I became the party's director of compliance, the Electoral Commission (EC) announced an investigation into whether we were reporting our donations properly and for the next few years we were in a virtually perpetual state of conflict with them. We used to have meetings about them almost every week, usually to discuss how to bat off the latest accusation about the poor state of our record keeping or some omission in our reporting.

In 2003, I decided we had to smarten up our act. I started organising seminars for our MPs and their staff to ensure they knew what their obligations were regarding donations they received, and to ensure they were clear about what type of work could legitimately be funded by the taxpayer. I also talked to them about data protection, something many of them didn't really bother about. I was seriously concerned that sooner or later someone would find themselves being criminalised, and felt that it was part of our duty of care to our MPs to help them avoid the pitfalls.

When Matt became General Secretary in 2003, he launched a mission to sort out our relationship with the EC. Like me, he did not think we should be permanently at war with them, and so we began to build bridges. I did a great deal of work on this, holding regular meetings with EC officials, and by 2004 we were getting on very well. I had begun to build a reputation for myself across the party as someone who was very aware of legal risks and knew how to ensure we stayed on the right side of the law. I suspect that our 2005 election return – that is, the official record of the donations we received and how much we spent, which must be sent to the EC – was the first accurate one we'd ever filed. It's not that previous ones were deliberately falsified, just that systems had not been in place before to ensure the information that was submitted was correct. But I wasn't able to control and prevent everything that could land us in trouble, as I was to discover to my cost.

In April 2005, about two weeks before the general election, a story appeared in *The Guardian* revealing that the Tories had been taking loans from supporters. They were said to be building up millions of pounds of debt by relying on credit from wealthy backers, using the cash to finance their election campaign. The piece claimed the Tories were facing a crisis after the election, when most of the money– a reported £8 million – would have to be repaid.

There was nothing illegal about this. If the loans were below market rates, they would have to be declared to the EC, but commercial loans did not have to be registered in this way. However, it was interesting that the Tories were having to resort to this method of funding their campaign, and there was a discussion at one of our morning meetings about whether we should attack them for it. Matt said he didn't think it would be a good idea and asked to speak to me privately after the meeting.

'Just to let you know, we've taken loans from supporters too, so we can't attack them,' he told me matter-of-factly, when everyone had left the room.

I didn't react with particular alarm, though I was surprised I didn't know about it. 'How were the loans arranged?' I asked him, curious.

Matt told me he had approached someone on my team who had a formal legal background, and asked them about whether or not it would be possible for the party to take loans from supporters. Following that conversation, legal contracts had been drawn up for use with lenders.

It was two weeks before polling day and I didn't feel it was the time to press for more detail or have a hissy fit about being left out of the loop. However, Matt was obviously a bit anxious, as he asked me to prepare a 'line' for the media just in case we were asked about it. For the time being, the subject was closed.

A week after the 2005 election, Matt and I got together for a coffee and he announced he was promoting me. I had been really hoping he was going to ask me to do a bigger job – I was very ambitious, and knew I wanted to be General Secretary at some point. I also knew he did not intend to stick around forever and therefore my chance to go for his job might come quite soon. I was hoping he would make me his deputy.

We took our mugs of coffee into the private meeting room.

'Peter, will you become director of finance?' Matt asked.

I was totally taken aback. It was definitely a bigger job than Deputy General Secretary, but it was not the job I expected, or wanted. 'I don't have any financial background!' I told him, trying not to sound shocked.

'It doesn't matter. You can bring people in. Our finances are incredibly political, and we need someone with a political head to be in charge of them,' he replied.

I could hardly turn it down, and it was certainly a promotion, putting me on the right track for the top job if Matt left, so I agreed, though I can't say I felt massively enthusiastic about it. It was a very daunting prospect. My title was to be Director of Finance and Compliance – meaning I would still have the responsibilities of my old role. I told Matt I would need a couple of weeks to prepare, and arranged to spend some time with a Labour-supporting firm of accountants. Soon after, my promotion was announced.

It was a period in which almost everyone else in the party was taking things easy. It's always the same after a general election – there is a lull, while everyone recovers from all the adrenalin and tries to recharge their batteries. For me, there was no such respite. All the election bills were pouring in, and I had to deal with them, as well as sort our official return for the EC.

My predecessor in the finance job had been a highly qualified accountant, and I got the impression he was a little insulted that someone like me with no experience was taking over. About ten days before I officially started, he began talking me through exactly what I was inheriting.

It boiled down to two things. Firstly, we needed to find roughly another £8 million to pay our election bills. We had maxed out our £6 million overdraft, £1 million of which had to be repaid quickly; and the bills had to be settled fast. It seemed that with a fair wind, we could muddle through until the end of the year, but it would not take much to bring the whole pack of cards tumbling down. It did not take a genius to work out that we were in pretty deep shit. Secondly, the loans Matt had mentioned a few weeks earlier amounted to £9 million, with a further £4 million scheduled to come before the end of the year. I listened to these figures in shocked silence.

Among the paperwork my predecessor handed me for my new role was a file containing the loan agreements. When I saw the contents I was very surprised. The documentation for £9 million worth of loans was contained in a scrappy little file. It was hard to believe this was all we had. Paperwork for some of the loans was missing – either it had been lost, or nobody had chased up the signed copy of the agreement from the lender. Others forms were undated or unsigned.

I remember walking back to my desk, thinking, 'Fucking hell. Is that it? Is that really all the paperwork for loans of £9 million?' It was completely shambolic.

I went to see Matt. 'I've just got a sense of the size of those loans. I'm not sure I'd have taken up your kind offer of employment if I had realised then what I know now,' I said grimly.

I was not entirely joking – clearly we had a huge problem and now it was my responsibility to sort it out. How the hell were we going to repay it all?

Matt seemed pretty relaxed, though it was clear the NEC did not know. It had never been raised officially, and Matt said Jack Dromey, the party treasurer, did not know.

This was not as strange as it sounds. The position of party treasurer was largely symbolic and Jack did not actually get involved in day-to-day issues about party funding. The legal treasurer of the party was the General Secretary.

Over the summer, Matt became increasingly worried about the loans. I clearly remember NEC meetings during which party finance was discussed and our £13 million secret was never raised. NEC officers were simply kept out of the loop. Legally, we were doing nothing wrong, but I was very uncomfortable about the situation. I'd like to say that my unease was because I am honourable and felt the NEC deserved to know, but actually I was just scared. I simply could not see how we could service such huge debt. I hated the fact that so few people knew about it.

In mid-July 2005, Matt and I met the party's chief fundraiser, Michael Levy, at his flat to talk about donors and lenders. Matt met him fairly regularly to discuss potential financial supporters, Michael working through a list of names and outlining what he thought they might give. During the meeting Matt asked Michael directly whether he thought any of the people who had given us loans would convert them into donations.

'I don't know,' Michael replied.

The meeting wrapped up, and Matt and I jumped in a taxi back to the office. Matt's mood had changed dramatically. He seemed very tense and it was obvious his mind was elsewhere. I assumed he was beginning to focus on what we were going to do about the loans. As the cab picked its way through the rush hour traffic back to Victoria, I pointed out to him that at some stage we were going to have to come clean to the NEC. 'We do have a bit of a problem here, because when we produce our annual accounts for the year, we will have to list these loans. Whatever the plan is for dealing with them, there is no way we can just leave them off the balance sheet,' I said.

Matt muttered something non-committal and I left it at that. Around the same time, he was telling the wider Labour Party how well our finances had been managed for the general election. For example, he gave a presentation to regional staff on short-term contracts, many of whom were expecting to be made redundant, announcing that they could stay put. There are always staff cutbacks after a general election, but we didn't lose nearly as many as had been anticipated. I'm not suggesting Matt was deliberately misleading anyone: clearly, for whatever reason, he genuinely believed we would be able to repay the loans if they were not converted into donations. But I felt very uneasy, perhaps because I had not been involved in arranging the loans and was not privy to the expectations of the lenders.

It was a difficult time as I tried to find my feet in my new job with the anxiety of the loans always hanging over me. I really didn't understand finance and it was a steep learning curve. I didn't know what was really going on with the loans and didn't feel I'd necessarily been told everything I needed to know. However, anyone could see that we had massively overextended ourselves.

Matt went on holiday for the rest of the summer and when he returned in September, he announced he was going to resign in December. In what was a massive step for me, I decided to apply for his job. I knew I would have to fight for it and I did not underestimate just how much time and energy it would take to win.

The weeks that followed were completely dominated by my campaign for the job, and there was little time to worry about anything else. However, the loans were always at the back of my mind.

At the end of November 2005, I was appointed General Secretary. A bizarre meeting with Matt before he left was a worrying portent of how toxic the loans were going to become. It was early December and

Matt had invited a small group of senior party staff for a farewell lunch in an Italian restaurant in London's West End: myself, Roy, Alicia, Vic Gould, Hilary Perrin and Luke Bruce, who was head of policy at the time. We were due to meet at 1 p.m. Around 10 a.m., Matt called me into the small meeting room, saying he'd just phoned Ruth and asked her to come over. He wanted to speak to us both together.

Ruth arrived looking worried. Matt didn't bother inviting us to sit down. 'I just want to say to the two of you that the decision to take loans was nothing to do with me. It was not my responsibility. I am going to put it in writing, so it is on record,' he said abruptly. He didn't say whose decision it was.

Ruth and I were gobsmacked, feeling we'd been dropped in it. It felt as if Matt knew a shit storm was brewing, but it was no longer his problem. Matt and I shared a taxi to his farewell lunch and we stopped outside Downing Street to deliver his statement distancing himself from the loans.

Not surprisingly, it was a pretty weird lunch. He was all jolly, getting the party credit card out to pay for extra bottles of wine. I remember thinking, rather uncharitably, that it was easy for him to put the bill on the party's credit card, but I was going to have to find a way to pay for it.

## CIVIL WAR

As I embarked on my new role as General Secretary, my worries were not confined to the loans. A major controversy was building in the media about links between donations to the party and the awarding of political honours, and it was beginning to look very messy.

The idea that Tony had been rewarding donors with peerages had been around for a while. Over the summer, the *News of the World* had published a story revealing that all of those who had donated more than £1 million to the Labour Party had received a knighthood or peerage. The SNP leader, Alex Salmond, branded it 'an incredible abuse of the system' and coined the phrase 'cash for honours'. He accused Tony of 'stuffing' the Lords with his cronies instead of modernising and reforming the upper chamber as we'd promised in 1997.

The story largely went away until late October, when the *Independent on Sunday* published an article revealing that the Prime Minister planned to reward a 'clutch of millionaire donors' with seats in the Lords. The piece was based on a leaked list of names Tony was nominating for peerages, including Chai Patel, who ran the Priory clinics; Sir Gulam Noon, who made a fortune from ready-made curries; and Sir David Garrard, a millionaire property developer. All of them were high rollers who had donated very large sums to the party. The article highlighted Garrard's sponsorship of the government's flagship academy schools programme. It also mentioned Barry Townsley, a millionaire stockbroker who had not only given us money but also sponsored a city academy.

The story caused a storm, with opposition MPs queuing up to accuse Tony of corruption, cronyism and sleaze. Norman Baker, the Lib Dem MP, claimed the process of appointments to the Lords had 'fallen into total disrepute'. 'The people with the biggest chequebooks are first in the queue. This makes Lloyd George look clean,' he puffed. The House of Lords Appointments Commission, responsible for vetting nominations, was summoned before the parliamentary standards commissioner to discuss the situation.

The awarding of honours was handled entirely by No. 10, and nobody at HQ had ever been involved. However, I knew some of the donors involved in the row had also given us loans. If the existence of our loans became public, it would not take a huge leap for someone to suggest a link with the awarding of honours.

I had confided in Roy about our £13 million secret, having appointed him director of finance when I became General Secretary. We had been trying to work out a strategy for getting it all out into the open. I was terrified about suddenly telling the NEC we had borrowed millions of pounds they didn't know about, and had decided the best approach was to go through the NEC's audit committee first. I knew they would react badly but it had to be done. Subsequently John Prescott asked me why I didn't tell him about the loans earlier, and with hindsight he was right. It was a mistake to try to contain something that was not containable, and he could have helped defuse the situation. I suppose at the time I felt I was just about on top of things – though I was already having sleepless nights.

That Christmas Vilma and I went to Florida with the kids. We had three foster children who had been with us for ages, including a ten-month old baby who had been with us since birth, and two little lads who were leaving us soon because adoptive parents had been found. It was supposed to be a special holiday for us all before the boys left. We had great fun, though I have to say Christmas Day at Disneyland is a challenging experience for grown-ups. It seemed like every other bugger in Florida had turned up, and there was a near riot in one of the food halls as families battled for seats. Though the kids had an amazing time, Vilma and I were so tired and irritated by the afternoon that we didn't even stay for the fireworks over the Magic Kingdom. I remember seeing the display reflected in the hire car mirrors as we drove away and feeling distinctly relieved we were out of there.

Throughout the holiday I was massively distracted. I was scared about the situation at work. I knew I would have to go back and deal with the financial wasteland I had inherited, and that harsh decisions, including redundancies, lay ahead. I was pissed off that I had been put into a position where I had to start my new job like this and I was worried about getting the existence of the loans into the public domain. The whole 'cash for honours' issue was bubbling too, and though I was not overly worried about it at this stage, it was not something I could ignore.

A few days after Christmas it emerged that the House of Lords Appointments Commission was blocking several of Tony's nominations. Newspapers reported that the decision was being taken because the organisation had a duty to 'satisfy itself that the person would be a credible nominee irrespective of any payments made to a political party'. On 15 January 2006 there was another blow when the *Sunday Times* published a sensational report claiming people who sponsored city academies could obtain honours and peerages in return.

It followed an undercover investigation by the paper. It was probably the most damning evidence yet of 'cash for honours' and our political opponents lost no time in ramping it up to the max. A head of steam was building.

The Appointments Commission spent some weeks deliberating over what to do about the nominations, leaving the donors in limbo while the media crawled all over their affairs. Not surprisingly, they began to turn against us.

Barry Townsley (who had given us a loan of £1 million) removed himself from the list of nominees, indicating he'd had enough, while Chai Patel exploded following false reports that the Appointments Commission was investigating the tax status. 'There is more than one occasion when I have thought, and wished – and my children have said – that I hadn't donated [to the Labour Party]. I have never wanted anything for this money,' he told the media.

The whole situation was a mess. On 10 March, *The Times* published a story accusing No. 10 of failing to tell the Appointments Commission that David Garrard had given the Labour Party a £1 million loan.

This was the moment I'd dreaded. Our loans were now in the public domain, and opposition politicians were asking awkward questions.

The sharp Lib Dem Treasury spokesman Matthew Oakeshott quickly cottoned on. 'We should be told the amount of loans that individuals have made and how much is still outstanding. Are loans repaid if people do not get peerages? Are they not repaid if people do get peerages? What interest rate is charged?' he told the press.

There was now no escape from putting the NEC in the picture. There was shocked silence when I admitted the scale of our borrowings at the next meeting of NEC officers. 'I know it's a shocking figure, but there's no immediate crisis,' I said calmly. 'We are not suddenly going to have to find £13 million. There's plenty of time for us to negotiate and talk to the individual lenders. They're all friends of the party, and I'm really optimistic that many of them will agree to convert the loans into donations over the coming months.'

I pointed out that our auditors knew about the situation. It did not really occur to me to point out that I had had nothing to do with the loans. There seemed little point in blaming others, and I felt I had simply had to take responsibility. I tried to reassure the NEC but frankly they were livid, and they were absolutely right to be. JP was particularly cross because he felt he could have helped if he'd known. I was desperate to avoid a sense of panic, and I did what I could to make the NEC officers feel I was on top of things. It was agreed that a full meeting of the party's business board would be held two days later to discuss how to handle the situation.

I spent most of the following day sitting in Jack's offices at the T&G's headquarters in north London, going through the party's finances with him and Roy. It was the first time I knew of that Jack had asked to see paperwork, indicating the level of concern. It seemed a constructive meeting, and when we wrapped up at 3 p.m. I felt a little more relaxed.

At the meeting of the party's business board the following day there was much heated discussion. Members understandably needed to offload their anger at being kept in the dark about the loans. Though I became the focus of some of the attacks, I kept calm, understanding that people needed to lash out at someone. After all the shouting, it was agreed that Jack and I would jointly give a prepared report about the loans to a full meeting of the NEC the following week. We decided it was best if the party made no public statement on the loans before then. Importantly, we agreed that when the time came for us to comment, there should only be one public statement, issued by the NEC and the business board.

The meeting finished at 4.15 p.m. It had been a tough couple of days, and Jack and I, who had been working really well together, went for a cup of coffee in the meeting room in Victoria Street. I felt he had been very constructive. We talked through what our report to the NEC might look like, and he was very supportive. He sympathised with what a hard few weeks I'd had, and said I'd handled it very well. He said he was sure we'd give a good account of ourselves at the full meeting of the NEC. Jack left Victoria Street at 4.45.

I spent the rest of the afternoon catching up on messages and emails. Just after 7.00, as I was thinking about calling it a day, I received a call from one of the press officers, who was based in another part of the building. 'You'd better come round,' she said, in a voice that could only mean trouble.

I hurried over to see what was up. To my amazement, Comrade Jack was live on *Channel 4 News*, blowing a gasket about the loans.

'No. 10 must have known about the loans. I'm the treasurer of the Labour Party and to be absolutely frank I don't believe the Labour Party has been sufficiently respected by No. 10. What I want to do is assert the democratic integrity of the Labour Party,' he spluttered.

I stared at the TV in disbelief. Was this the same man who that afternoon had agreed with the rest of us that no statement should be issued for the time being? Was this the same Jack who had just had a cup of coffee with me and said he thought everything would be okay? The same Jack who'd left my office less than three hours ago, apparently satisfied with the strategy we'd all agreed?

Unfortunately he was just warming up. That night, he toured the TV studios, turning what was already a really difficult situation into a full-blown crisis that threatened to engulf us all. 'Whoever I need to talk to to get to the bottom of this, I will do precisely that. The party, its institutions and its democracy need to be respected, including by No. 10 . . . We have once and for all to end any notion that there is cash for favours in our political culture,' he said. In comments that were guaranteed to massively increase the heat on Tony, he suggested he was ready to question the Prime Minister about what had happened if necessary.

I was gobsmacked. What had happened to Jack between 4.45, when he left Victoria Street, having agreed our strategy, and 7.00, when he got star billing on *Channel 4 News*? To whom did he speak, and (since we had left on such good terms that afternoon) why hadn't he warned me that he was planning to go nuclear?

Others were equally shocked. JP phoned me on my mobile. 'Have you seen what that bastard is up to?' he shouted. 'What the fuck is he doing? Wait till I fucking speak to him!'

I didn't even try to calm him down. What was the point? He was absolutely right. For whatever reason Jack had gone behind our backs, and created the impression there had been some huge conspiracy.

I could not see how this approach was going to be good for anyone except possibly Gordon. Later, rumours swirled in No. 10 of a furious bust-up between the Chancellor and the Prime Minister. One of Tony's senior aides told me Gordon threatened to use the crisis to oust him. 'I'll bring you down with sleaze,' the Chancellor was said to have yelled. Word of the bust-up quickly spread through Downing Street, and the Chancellor's alleged threat became common currency.

To what extent was Jack acting on Gordon's orders or encouragement when he took to the airwaves that night? I cannot be sure. Gordon had told me privately that he had no influence over Jack. However, when I told people in No. 10 about this comment, they just laughed. When I told Tony, he looked skywards in a 'believe that if you want to' way.

Events had spiralled out of my control and there was nothing more I felt we could do that night. The press office sorted out a holding statement for the media confirming that Jack had been unaware of the loans when they were taken out. At about 8 p.m., Roy and I decided we'd had enough and headed for the pub. The place was packed and there was nowhere to sit, so we found a pillar and slumped against it, completely drained. Both of us knew this could not end well. Jack had portrayed us as a party at war with itself. Internally and externally, we were now facing an epic crisis.

We spent the following day fending off a relentless barrage of questions about loans, donations and peerages, our inexperienced press team performing miracles keeping our heads above water. All day we ducked and dived, batting off demands for information we did not have or could not release. The weekend did not bring much relief and I spent most of the time fretting about the looming NEC meeting.

In fact, it went better than expected: there was a sense that the world had turned against us, and now we would pull together and fight our way out. Tony was fantastic, saying he knew about the loans. I am not sure whether this was true, and even if it was I doubt he had any idea of the scale. Yet he sat there and said he took full responsibility. He was very robust, talking about how financing elections was very difficult, and that sometimes tough or unpopular decisions had to be made. It was all constructive stuff, and I left the meeting feeling relieved.

By then I should have learned that in this job, just when you thought things could not get worse, they usually did.

## UNDER CAUTION

It sounds shamefully blasé, but nobody in the Labour Party was that concerned when some bloke most of us had never heard of decided to report us to the police.

I had only just sat back down at my desk following the NEC meeting when Angus MacNeil, an SNP MP, popped up on TV saying he'd complained to the Metropolitan Police and the Director of Public Prosecutions that we had broken the law. The allegation was that we had 'sold' honours in return for loans, an offence under a 1925 act passed following the sale of peerages by Lloyd George.

I remember thinking it wasn't particularly serious. Almost everyone at Westminster saw it as a political stunt. We'd probably have tried the same thing in their shoes.

I had a more immediate problem: what to do about the growing clamour for the names of our lenders. Though I had given the list to Jack, I had not distributed it to the NEC. We had a contract with the lenders which stated that as the money they were giving us was a loan it did not have to be publicly disclosed. This put us in a difficult position: if we revealed their identities, we would be in breach of contract, and they would be within their rights to demand their money back right away. If we did not, it would look as if we had something to hide.

I spoke to Michael Levy and David Hill from No. 10 to try to work out what to do. Michael was against us releasing the names, feeling it was a kind of betrayal, but I argued that we had no choice. It was obvious the press would dig, and there was likely to be a damaging drip-drip of names if we didn't put them into the public domain ourselves. Michael could see my logic and started hitting the phones, trying to track all the lenders down to explain the situation and persuade them to allow us to publish their identities.

The process was a nightmare – many of the lenders were overseas and very difficult to contact. One individual was holidaying on a boat off the Galapagos Islands and took an age to reach, but we could not release the names piecemeal – it had to be all at once or none.

At some point, I asked Gerald Shamash, one of the party's solicitors, to send me a brief on the Honours (Prevention of Abuses) Act 1925, the law MacNeil was claiming we might have breached. Though I was not worried about it, I obviously needed to know what the legislation said.

The atmosphere in the office was very tense. For the first time that week, I saw how panic can set in among staff working in an open plan office. It was not the prospect of a police inquiry, which at this stage was not being taken seriously, but rather the sense that we were under siege, with every day bringing some kind of fresh onslaught. I was conscious that people were looking to see whether I looked calm and in control. If I did, it seemed to rub off on them. It was an enormous psychological effort to maintain this composure for fourteen hours a day, when inside I was very agitated. By the time I returned home at night, I simply had nothing left to give, and I must have been dreadful company for Vilma. It was a very rough time, both at work and at home, as all my energy went into handling the crisis.

We had all been so nonchalant that it was a huge shock when at 6 p.m. on 21 March, Scotland Yard announced it was investigating MacNeil's claims. The Specialist Crime Directorate was reported to be looking into three complaints relating to alleged breaches of the 1925 act, in relation to loans-for-peerages allegations. There was panic at HQ. I was already exhausted and preoccupied by the cascade of bills landing on the office doormat that I knew we could not pay. I felt as if I was trying to doggy-paddle across the Channel, always on the brink of going under as another killer wave crashed over me.

Around a week later I received a letter from the Met confirming that they had decided to investigate and requesting a number of documents, such as NEC minutes and paperwork on nominations to the House of Lords. I didn't know anything about how individuals were nominated for the Lords, and knew we didn't have any records relating to the process at Victoria Street. But I passed the letter on to Gerald, and he assembled everything from our files that seemed relevant.

A little later, he rang me. 'Just to let you know, I've picked up a rumour that they're going to interview three or four people,' he said.

'Oh, right,' I replied, surprised. It was all happening so quickly. 'Who?'

'I don't know, but I don't think they would want to interview you. Perhaps they'll want to speak to you at some point, but I can't see why they'd start with you,' Gerald answered.

My secretary Anouska Gregorek told me she had cleared my diary for that Friday, and pretty much ordered me not to come into work.

She knew I was frazzled. Vilma was thrilled when I told her we were going to have a long weekend, and we decided to use my Friday off for a crazy day out, just the two of us, at Chessington World of Adventures, mucking about on the rides.

We had been there about an hour when Marianna rang. 'We've had a letter from the police. They want to interview you under caution,' she said.

I moved away from Vilma so she couldn't hear. 'When?' I asked, shocked. My mouth was dry.

'We need to contact them to arrange a date,' she replied.

She didn't have any more details, and Vilma was hovering, so I hung up. My mind was racing as I tried to work out what it all meant. Blissfully unaware of what had just happened, Vilma dragged me off to the Vampire Ride, a huge roller-coaster. As we hurtled along at 45mph, I decided the obvious thing to do was call Gerald. However when we got off I discovered my phone had fallen out of my pocket somewhere along the ride. I became ridiculously agitated, stomping about and cursing myself for losing it at this of all moments. All I could think of was that I needed to speak to Gerald, and now my mobile had disappeared. Vilma was bemused and asked me why I was getting so worked up. 'It's only a phone,' she said, reasonably.

So I told her. She was quite calm – neither of us had any idea at that stage what lay ahead. I was quite clear that I had not done anything wrong. All but one of the loans, for £2 million, which I signed off myself, had been in place by the time I became General Secretary, and there was no doubt they were legal. Yet I suddenly felt massively scared and vulnerable. I knew I had to keep calm and pretend everything was okay, but I actually wanted to run away. Chessington World of Adventures had lost its appeal, and our day together, the first we had had alone for about eighteen months, was spoiled.

I spent the whole weekend worrying and wondering who to tell. I was the only person Gerald knew of who was being interviewed under caution and despite knowing I had done nothing wrong, I was genuinely frightened. I wanted to tell Dad, but couldn't bring myself to. He was proud of my job, as was Mum. They had never been in trouble with the police and neither had I, so I was embarrassed and worried about him being ashamed of me.

I didn't know who I should tell at work and was wondering if I could even continue as General Secretary of the party if I was under a police investigation. I decided I'd better tell No. 10, but the only person who knew at that stage at party HQ was Marianna.

I felt humiliated and very angry. I had taken the job knowing the loans were going to be an issue, but it had never for one second occurred to me that they would be a legal issue. I was worried about my children too. The Met seemed to be leaking a lot of information and I felt it could only be a matter of time before my situation was exposed. I was a proud dad, proud of my job, and I knew the kids were proud of me too. How would they feel if they discovered I was being investigated for a crime? Meanwhile, Vilma buried her head in the sand, pretending it was not happening. None of this helped our already strained relationship.

I went into the office as normal on the Monday having had virtually no sleep all weekend. I remember very vividly sitting in the meeting room and hearing the wail of a police siren, and honestly thinking the police car was coming for me. My heart pounded as if it would burst.

That week, I explained what was going on to Jo Murray, our head of press, asking her not to tell anyone else on the team. I also told Roy, Alicia and Hilary. I felt better once Roy knew – at least there was now someone I could talk to. Every night at home, I would log onto the computer and check the first editions of the papers to see if news of my situation had leaked. Fridays and Saturdays were the worst – I knew the Sunday papers would be digging on the story and I was living in dread of a call from a journalist.

About a week after we received the police letter, a date was fixed for my interview. I was to be questioned at Gerald's office in Waterloo. This was a relief in itself, as I'd discovered through a lot of late-night Googling that interviews under caution can take place at a time and place of the police's choosing. At least they were negotiating.

In the run-up to the event, they made various requests for further information. My attitude was always that we should be completely frank and tell them whatever they wanted to know. Gerald on the other hand seemed to think it was his duty to the party to file anything the police wanted at the last minute, something I was afraid would wind them up. At one point, the police wrote to Hazel Blears, who was then chair of the party, complaining that we were being obstructive.

'What do I do about it?' she asked me worriedly.

'I think it's Gerald,' I replied. 'He tends to give them stuff at the last possible moment. I think he thinks that's the best way to go about things from the party's point of view, but I don't think it's helping.'

The police asked for access to our secret email system, but we didn't have one. A number of stories appeared in the press about us refusing to let them look at the network, but in truth all we used was Lotus Notes, a perfectly ordinary email system found in millions of offices. All this worried me even more – the last thing I wanted was to give the police any excuse to arrest me. I feared that if they thought we were being obstructive they might pull me in to 'protect evidence'.

Around a week before my interview Michael rang asking me whether Gerald had fully prepared me. He had started to consult his own lawyers, since he felt he might also be questioned at some stage. He gave me a real grilling about what Gerald had done to ensure I was ready, urging me to hire another lawyer if I was not entirely happy. However, I trusted Gerald and didn't see any reason to instruct anyone else. He had appointed two barristers to advise, and I spent an hour with all three of them, preparing a formal statement for the police. I lived in fear of coming out of Gerald's office and finding myself in a blaze of flashbulbs, but amazingly it never happened. It was all very surreal. Though I was at the centre of a huge story, nobody in the media had cottoned on.

During this time I hung on to Gerald's every word, always desperate for any snippet of information he might have gleaned from the police or his legal contacts. I would try to squeeze minute details out of him from the conversations he was having with the detectives, such as how their voices sounded. Whenever he came into HQ he looked very worried, and I felt that all the staff were watching this performance. It didn't do anything to calm the atmosphere in the office.

Three days before I was due to be interviewed, I received a folder of material we had been anxiously awaiting from the police. It was all part of the legal disclosure process, under which detectives tell suspects what evidence they have collected. Gerald went to pick it up from Scotland Yard and came into the office with it under his arm, striding over to me dramatically with his overcoat swinging and the usual worried expression on his face. I found his attitude irritating, so I put on an air of nonchalance, fiddling about with a few things on my desk to keep him waiting. But my palms were sweaty with fear when he handed me the file.

In the event it was a complete anti-climax. All the ring binder contained was copies of the nine loan agreements. The file had had such a build-up – the police had told us we could keep it for just twenty-four hours – that I really expected it to contain some kind of smoking gun. I should have been relieved, but strangely I was almost disappointed. 'Is this the best they can do? I have all this stuff on my computer anyway!' I thought.

The morning of my interview, a Friday, was like any other in our household. The alarm went off at 5.45 a.m., Radio 5 came on, and I jumped in the shower before the kids all started fighting for it. My daughter Ivanna always takes longer than anyone else and uses up all the hot water, so I moved fast. There was the usual chaos as Vilma and I sorted breakfast for the little ones, me taking the usual hit of baby food on my suit, and I fed and watered our chickens and put the recycling outside before helping Vilma pack the older children off to school. Nobody, chickens included, seemed that bothered about what I was about to face.

'Have a good day,' Vilma said breezily as I left, as if it were like any other Friday. I remember thinking how bizarre it was that she didn't even wish me good luck. I took the train to Waterloo and headed for Gerald's office.

'Is Gerald in yet?' I asked the receptionist.

'Yes but he's busy,' she said, in a pointed kind of way.

'I'm Peter,' I announced.

'Ooh,' she replied, in a very serious voice, 'I think he's in with the gentlemen now. Have a seat.'

A few minutes later, Gerald popped out, wearing his best concerned face. 'Are you okay?' he asked me.

We were due to start at 9.30 a.m., and it was about 9.29 and a half.

'Shall we have a cup of coffee?' he suggested.

'Shouldn't we just go in?' I replied.

Gerald shrugged. 'Let's keep them waiting for five minutes,' he said.

As we headed to his office canteen, he told he he'd received a letter from the police, questioning whether he should be representing me.

'Oh?' I said, surprised he hadn't mentioned it before.

'Yeah. Let me just make a call,' Gerald replied easily, and with me just standing there, and the police waiting upstairs, he dialled some barrister to see if they thought it was a problem. I stood wondering what would happen if the barrister agreed there was an issue.

In the event the barrister thought it was fine and so, ten minutes late, we headed over to the room where the police were waiting to get started. Gerald pulled down the blinds so nobody outside could see what was going on.

The police were in plain clothes, sitting at a table with a huge tape recording machine in front of them. I felt like I was in an episode of *The Bill*.

I sat down and Gerald announced he also wanted to record the interview. The officers agreed, but when they tested their own equipment it didn't work, so the session was postponed for twenty minutes while one of them went off to find another machine. It was all quite chatty and informal at this point and I think we had a bit of banter about sport. But when the officer returned with the new equipment, the atmosphere suddenly changed and became very official. I was hooked up to a microphone and asked to sign various labels for the tapes. They made two copies of each recording: one for storage, one to be used as evidence.

When we were ready to start, one of the officers gave the official spiel. 'Interview with Mr Peter Watt, General Secretary of the Labour Party. Also present in the room is Mr Gerald Shamash, representing Mr Watt. Before we start, I must caution you that anything you say now could later be used in evidence against you in court.'

Though I still felt like I was in some TV drama it was a very sobering moment. Questioning began at 10 a.m. and finished about 5½ hours later. At one point, the police ran out of tapes and had to go out to restock. We broke for lunch, during which the officers revealed they had initially expected to work on the investigation for only around ten days. Now it was clear it was going to drag on for months. I think they had approached the inquiry as if it were a sort of fraud case which could be dealt with swiftly. Instead they were confronted by the sort of political chaos that takes months to unravel.

The bizarre thing was that by the time we stopped for lunch I was almost enjoying myself. Like most men I love talking about myself and I sort of got into a rhythm. However, every time they changed the tape I was cautioned again, so there was no forgetting this was for real.

It gradually transpired from their line of questioning that the police thought I'd cooked up the paperwork for the loans after people started asking awkward questions. Not surprisingly they thought it was odd that some of the paperwork wasn't properly signed and dated and that documents were missing. The issue was whether the loans were real loans, the suspicion being that they would have been converted into donations as soon as the lenders had received their peerages.

The police would say things like 'Do you really expect us to believe that you had £5 million worth of loans handed over with missing hard copies of the written agreements? That seems incredible.'

'Yes, it's incredible,' I would answer. I'd been pretty surprised about it myself. 'But that's how it is. You can come and have a look at the computer versions of these loan agreements if you like. You will be able to see on our computer system when these documents were created.'

I knew we had computer files that would torpedo their theory. Though the paperwork was scrappy, I was able to tell the police honestly that they were real loans and had been accruing interest in the normal way. 'They feel pretty commercial to me, from where I am sitting, trying to pay the bills and having to tell the lenders we don't even have enough money to pay their interest,' I said.

Uncomfortable conversations between us and the lenders had

certainly been taking place. We regularly had to ring them, cap in hand, explaining we simply did not have any money, and they would agree to wait.

Not surprisingly, once the furore started, the lenders were very annoyed and the pressure to repay the money intensified. At a time when I was in what I felt was a pretty unfair position myself, I was also having to try and smooth things over with the lenders, who were justifiably furious at the way their generosity was being repaid. I was basically dealing with it all myself, as everyone else in the party had run a mile.

The police also asked about my relationship with Tony. 'Do you meet him? What do you talk to him about? Do you ever talk to him about money?' they wanted to know.

'Yes, I tell him we're broke, and he tells me not to worry,' I replied.

They asked how people were nominated for peerages, and I replied truthfully that I had no idea. They even asked if I had ever nominated anyone myself, something I would have found funny if the circumstances weren't so serious.

It quickly became clear that they did not understand how government decisions were made, imagining there was a clear structure when the reality is far messier. When I tried to explain what it was really like, I think they thought I was trying to be clever.

'Are you expecting us to believe that you are General Secretary of the Labour Party and yet you are not even consulted about who is going to be nominated for the Lords?' they asked, incredulous.

But of course I was not. It was absolutely nothing to do with us at HQ.

I tried to explain the cut-throat world in which I worked. 'The truth is, everyone has got an agenda here. Jack Dromey says he's the treasurer of the Labour Party and should have known about the loans, but actually, I am legally the treasurer – legally, it is my responsibility. He is running an agenda, and it's all about undermining Tony,' I said.

It was reckless, but it was what I believed, and I could be totally honest in the privacy of that interview room. I remember thinking on my way home, 'If this gets to court it's going to make for a pretty interesting situation when everyone hears me having a go at Jack.' In a funny sort of way, though, it was nice to get everything off my chest. I had a real sense that the police were barking up the wrong tree and that was quite comforting.

When they'd finally run out of questions, they thanked me, mentioning that they might want to speak to me again. I had given them names of another eight people they had probably never considered who could back up what I'd said or offer further useful information. It seemed likely that some or all of those individuals would be contacted as witnesses if the police were as serious about getting to the bottom of things as they seemed. I came away from my interview knowing we were in for a long haul, but I was quietly confident my part in the saga was over. I felt I had given them everything I could.

That evening, I went for a couple of pints with Roy. The pub was packed and we knew quite a few of the punters were probably Tories, since they had an office just near ours at the time. I kept my voice down as I talked him through my bizarre day. By the time we left, I was feeling much more relaxed, and that weekend was one of the nicest Vilma and I had had for a long time.

On Monday morning, I was heading across Parliament Square to Downing Street when Gerald rang to say he'd just had a letter from the police asking if they could make an appointment to come in and copy our computer files.

I was quite relaxed about this – after all, I'd suggested they look – but I was surprised they felt it necessary. Gerald, on the other hand, was angry. 'I can't believe they're doing this!' he exclaimed. 'It's a waste of time. They're on a fishing expedition.'

I didn't like the idea of the police pitching up at the office and downloading whatever they wanted in full view of everyone, so I asked Gerald to see if it could be done discreetly. They agreed to come in at 7 a.m. one day, but in the event they were still faffing about at 9 a.m. when the staff were drifting in. Though they weren't in uniform it was obvious who they were and the whole thing was very embarrassing. They were struggling to replicate my laptop files, and eventually gave up, taking the machine away with them.

The more I thought about them rifling through my emails, the more uncomfortable I felt. I knew they could certainly find something to embarrass me if they tried hard enough – perhaps a message slagging off a high-profile colleague, or a private email to my wife. What I really wanted to do was to go through my entire computer records myself to see what I might have sent, but I was paranoid they would know I'd been searching through my files.

For weeks afterwards, I would stumble upon some email or other I'd sent in the past, and worry it might land us in it. For example, I had repeatedly told colleagues that I was hopeful we would never have to repay the loans, and there was at least one email in which I accidentally referred to a loan as a donation. It was entirely innocent, but it could certainly be used against me. It did show a looseness of attitude towards the money. I knew that if the police wanted to put pressure on me they could embarrass me. Thankfully they never did – but I was by no means off the hook.

## WAITING GAME

The police inquiry dragged on for what seemed like an eternity. We did our best to get on with our work, while wondering how it would all end. On several occasions Gerald had to go along to the Met to observe detectives looking through my emails. I had a right to have a lawyer present during this process.

Other Labour Party figures were questioned under caution, and soon we were all in the same boat: myself, Ruth, John McTernan and Michael Levy. These were people I worked with closely and you can imagine how awkward it all became, particularly when Ruth and John were advised to get separate lawyers. It was never articulated, but I sensed that they became a little suspicious of each other. You could hardly blame them. They could not possibly risk talking to each other about the case, and must have wondered whether they were telling the police the same things. It made working together very difficult, as we simply could not communicate naturally. Occasionally we would acknowledge what was going on, but generally we were too paranoid to discuss it in case we were accused of colluding over evidence. We were right to be wary.

For those who were not directly involved in the investigation, I don't think it seemed real. Colleagues could not relate to the genuine fear of ending up in the dock that haunted those of us who were questioned by the police. Meanwhile income to the party simply dried up. We had been expecting several million to be donated in the second half of 2006, and not a penny arrived. It was hardly surprising – who would want to be seen donating to the Labour Party amid such an overwhelming stench of sleaze?

One warm July evening, four months after the saga began, I was sitting in my back garden feeling dog tired when my phone rang. I had gone outside to escape from the chaos in the house and was sitting at the wooden table on our patio, head in my hands. It was Jane Hogarth, the party's head of high value fundraising.

'Peter, have you heard?'

'No?' I replied warily, my heart already sinking.

'Michael's going to be arrested tomorrow morning,' she said.

'Fucking hell,' I said, feeling the world closing in.

I was overcome with dread. I felt desperately sorry for Michael and his wife Gilda but my mind also switched to the state of the party's finances. I had been telling myself that the four or five million we were expecting would come in once it was all over. Clearly that wasn't going to happen any time soon and I had to make a major mental adjustment. The dire state of our finances hung over everything I did at work, and there wasn't even a chink of light at the end of the tunnel.

At work the next day, I told Marianna about Michael's arrest, also speaking confidentially to Jo in the press office.

'How do we respond?' Jo asked.

'We say something very nice about Michael, about what a great servant of the party he has been, and say we can't make any other comment because it's an ongoing police investigation,' I replied. I was determined that we make it clear we were not deserting him.

Of course there was no chance of this dramatic development not leaking and by noon that day – 12 July – the news bulletins were leading with the story. Reports of the arrest of 'Lord Cashpoint' blared out from the TV screens in Victoria Street, and you could almost smell the panic in the air. There was no way I could pretend everything was normal, so I called all the staff together for a pep talk.

'Right, I'm sure you've heard the news,' I said briskly. 'Obviously, our thoughts are with Michael and his wife. It must be awful for them. I am certain, as I am sure you are, that Michael is a man of the greatest integrity and has done nothing wrong. No matter what anyone else says, we the Labour Party stand square behind our friend.'

I was very emotional and I didn't mind the staff seeing it. I wanted them to see how angry and upset I was about what was happening. I knew it would be an excuse for people who didn't like the amazing work that Michael did for the party to have a go at him, and sure enough they did. Labour MPs and peers who had wanted to be his friend when he was riding high no longer wanted to know. 'Terrible what's happened to Michael, isn't it?' they'd say, with faux concern.

'Have you rung him?' I'd ask, and the answer would almost always be no.

Michael's arrest massively raised the stakes for all of us, and we became increasingly demoralised. I remember one particularly depressing and awkward meeting in No. 10, not long after his arrest – me, Jonathan Powell, Ruth and Michael himself. We had met to discuss how to repair our shattered relationship with our donors, but it was almost impossible to concentrate. Tony had gone off to Chequers, and for some reason we ended up sitting in his office. I remember Michael chomping gloomily on a banana, and all of us feeling really crap, because we couldn't come up with any ideas. It was clear that all that lay ahead for Tony was a long grim struggle to the finishing line of his premiership. I remember going home and crashing emotionally. I just didn't know where it would all end. Vilma and I were barely talking, not because we were arguing but because I had been in my own world for months. I think she probably thought it was 'just politics' and had no perception of how very real it all felt to me.

Just before Labour's annual conference in 2006, there was a new arrest: Sir Christopher Evans, one of the millionaires who'd given us a loan. Not surprisingly he was livid. 'If I'd thought for one moment I would be placed in this embarrassing and mind-boggling position I wouldn't have made the loan,' he told the media – and who could blame him?

I was in the States when Ruth was arrested. It was January 2007, and

I was on a trip organised by the US embassy. It hadn't exactly been the junket I'd hoped for. Because of the time difference between America and the UK, I'd been having to wake up about 4 a.m. for a teleconference with colleagues at HQ, and seemed to be spending most of my trip trying to deal with work stuff from across the Atlantic.

I was in a hotel in Lincoln, Nebraska. It was freezing outside, about 3 feet of snow on the ground. The US embassy had done me proud: I had been given a suite, with a kingsize bed and lounge. I had my BlackBerry plugged in and it was laid out on the bed with the alarm set. I was so attached to my BlackBerry I even slept with it.

It was 7.30 a.m. and I was still in bed when Marianna rang. Feeling dozy, I took the call lying down.

'I just wanted to let you know Ruth's been arrested,' she said flatly.

I sat bolt upright. Though I'd always feared this was coming, it was still a huge shock, especially when I heard how the police had gone about it. They'd taken her in a dawn raid, pitching up outside her house at 6.30 a.m. and dragging her off to the police station. It seemed ridiculously heavy handed and I felt a rush of anger on her behalf. Unlike Michael, who'd been warned he was going to be arrested and had been able to arrange the time, Ruth hadn't been given any notice and the first No. 10 knew about it was when she failed to turn up at work.

I asked Marianna to organise a teleconference between Gerald, myself and the two barristers the party had hired to work with Gerald on the case. I'd been going to see the barristers regularly. It was a form of therapy – I needed to hear them say they didn't think I would be arrested. But Ruth's arrest had very serious implications, suggesting the police were determined to make prosecutions. Worryingly, she had been lifted 'on suspicion of perverting the course of justice'. There were now sensational media reports of missing correspondence, and an attempted cover-up of the 'sale' of honours.

The manner of Ruth's arrest outraged Downing Street and the many Cabinet ministers, special advisers and MPs who knew and respected her. The view was that the police had massively overstepped the mark, especially as Ruth was a single woman living alone. There was an outpouring of support for her from colleagues, and senior Labour figures began openly briefing against the Met. This was dangerous territory, raising the temperature on both sides.

From that moment until the whole affair finally ended, I assumed that someone – Michael, John, Ruth, Jonathan, or even all four – would end up being prosecuted. The police seemed hell bent on getting a scalp. Our legal team, initially so bullish, was sounding less and less confident that it would come to nothing. Though I really didn't think I would end up being prosecuted myself, I feared that if the whole saga ended in a trial, I would be dragged into it in some way. Technically, I was still a suspect. Despite everything, Ruth, one of the brightest people around Tony, continued to offer him the soundest of advice, as if the dark cloud that hung over her simply was not there. I was amazed by her strength, and wondered how she managed to keep going so well.

During this period I was very anxious about Tony's position. All the people with whom I'd normally have discussed my concerns were involved in the case, and I didn't know where to turn. There were clearly serious implications for his future as Prime Minister if anybody was prosecuted, and we could hardly just ignore it. At the time, we were planning the transition from Tony to Gordon, and I remember a particularly uncomfortable conversation with Ben Wegg-Prosser and Ruth, in which we discussed the various scenarios under which Tony might leave. I questioned what would happen if there were prosecutions over 'cash for honours', and the consensus was that all bets would be off: Tony's future as Prime Minister would obviously be in serious doubt. Everyone in the party knew this, of course, and it was incredibly destabilising. It hardly made for an environment in which he could push through the reforms he still wanted to achieve before leaving office.

In April 2007, I was told in pretty unequivocal terms by the party's legal team that they expected prosecutions. I was not exactly surprised to hear it but as General Secretary of the party I now felt I had a duty to raise the toxic issue of what would happen to Tony if someone was charged. I needed to talk to someone I trusted about what we would do.

John Reid, then Home Secretary, was one of the few people not directly involved to whom I felt I could turn. He was massively loyal to the party, very clever, and highly respected by Tony. If we needed someone to have a difficult conversation with the Prime Minister, John was the man. I rang his special adviser and arranged a meeting in John's private office at the Home Office.

'John, I just need to share this with you. I know Tony is saying privately that though "cash for honours" is a real pain, nothing will come of it. I hope he's right, but I'm afraid there's a stronger likelihood of charges than he thinks. If something happens – if Ruth or John are charged, for example – it will happen in the next few weeks, and we will suddenly be in a very different place. I don't want to be the only person who's thought about it', I said.

'Is that what the party's lawyers are saying?' John asked thoughtfully.

'Yeah, they are now', I replied.

We talked for a bit, but didn't come to any conclusion about what would happen. I wasn't really expecting answers from him, and it was a relief to get it off my chest. Though I'm sure he took me seriously, I think he was still reassured by Tony's quiet confidence that everything would be okay. I promised to keep him posted on any developments.

Of all the suspects, John McTernan's position was perhaps the worst. His job was not at all secure, and he had a family to worry about. He was an employee of the Labour Party rather than a civil servant, and was worried that if the saga was not over by the time Tony left office he would find himself out of a job. He and Jack Dromey did not have a great relationship, and like Gordon, Jack was keen to downsize the number of special advisers the Labour Party was paying to be based at Downing Street. John was very worried about who else would employ him when he might be about to be prosecuted. We had some very honest conversations in which I reassured him that we would keep him on the payroll until the inquiry concluded. We had not always got on brilliantly, but I became quite close to him during this period. I felt very strongly that he had frequently stuck his neck out for the party, and felt he deserved better than to find himself in this position.

For political obsessives like the Westminster bloggers this was a fantastic time. They salivated over every tiny development in the case, often writing a load of inaccurate rubbish. The media feeding frenzy was being fuelled by a barrage of briefing by the police, MPs and friends of those who had been arrested or questioned. It became more and more hysterical. Then, just when we all thought it was never going to go away, the investigation was suddenly called off.

## FREE

It was a lovely warm evening, and I was sitting outside my local, the Chessington Oak, nursing a pint and scrolling through emails on my BlackBerry. It was July 2007, and if anything I was feeling more jittery about the inquiry than ever.

Gordon had just taken over as Prime Minister. Shortly before the transition, I had spoken to him privately about 'cash for honours', warning him that we strongly suspected someone would be prosecuted soon. Gerald had only recently received a letter from the police asking for more documentation relating to my role. I had just begun to feel a bit safer, having heard nothing from the Met about my involvement for months.

'That means the spotlight's back on me then?' I had asked Gerald wearily.

'Yes, it does,' he replied.

'Oh great, that's really reassuring,' I said sarcastically. I was annoyed that he did not sound more sympathetic.

It appeared that, far from winding down their operation, the police were upping the ante. Yet literally twenty-four hours after that conversation, the inquiry was over. I was just thinking about ordering another pint when John McTernan rang. 'Have you heard?' he asked, in a voice that I knew meant big news.

'What?' I said.

'The CPS [Crown Prosecution Service] are going to announce tomorrow that they're not going to press charges. They're dropping the case,' he said. He was weirdly calm.

'Oh my God!' I shouted, not calm at all and not caring who heard. 'That is incredible! You must be *so* relieved!'

But he seemed more angry than anything. I suppose it was the first time he could really let off steam about what he'd been through.

'I'm going to do *Newsnight* tonight,' he said grimly.

I wasn't sure this was a great idea. I suppose I was still super-cautious and wanted to be certain it was all over before any of us said anything we regretted. However, Downing Street had been officially informed the case was now closed, and John was determined to get his side of the story out.

'I never did anything wrong, and I want people to know that,' he said bullishly.

I understood how he felt. 'If that's what you need to do, then you should do it. It's such fantastic news,' I said.

The first person I rang was Ruth, who was very calm and relieved. Then I rang Damian McBride, Gordon's chief spin doctor. 'Just to let you know, John's doing *Newsnight*,' I told him. 'Can I suggest you let him do it? I think he's got every right to set the record straight, and I'm sure he won't say anything we'll have a problem with. He just wants people to know he never did anything wrong.'

'Does he have to?' Damian replied, not at all keen.

'Yes, he's been through hell. He does have to,' I answered firmly.

'Yeah, I suppose he has,' Damian said, knowing it was fair enough.

I went home a bit tipsy.

The next day, when the police officially announced their decision, was a bit of an anti-climax. Gerald bounded over to the office, very excited, and we all watched the police press conference on TV. But something was bothering me.

'Has John received a letter from the CPS?' I asked Gerald.

'Yes,' he answered.

'Does it say he's not a suspect any more? Because I haven't had one,' I replied.

Gerald shrugged it off. 'Oh, they've probably just forgotten,' he said.

It was illogical, but I started feeling panicky. I sat in my office in a cold sweat. 'I need something on paper,' I told Gerald, a thousand horrible scenarios racing through my head. Was I the only one not actually off the hook? Did they plan to go for me after all?

Gerald rang them up, and he was right – they had just forgotten. They rattled something off and faxed it over, and for the first time in months, I was finally able to relax. That Saturday, I went to Lord's cricket ground to see England play India as a guest of David Abrahams, a member of the party's '1000 Club' for donors. It was a gorgeous sunny day and I was finally feeling free. I took my seat in a stand that had no cover, and the hot summer sun beat down on me. I had a glass of champagne in my hand and my spirits soared. Soon I felt pleasantly woozy as I waited for David to arrive. The match had almost started when he texted, flustered, with profuse apologies. He was doing some voluntary work and couldn't escape. He was desperately embarrassed but I didn't care. For the first time, it had sunk in: the nightmare was over. I sipped my bubbly, and soaked up the hum of the crowd. It was the most fantastic day, and I went home feeling like a completely different person.

How ironic it seems now that this happiest of days was thanks to David. Little did I know then that my connection with him would land me in another police investigation. This time it would finish me.

# 6. ON THE STUMP

When everything else was going wrong, it was the thrill of fighting election campaigns that kept me going. Sometimes we were up, sometimes we were down, but there was one constant: our objective was to make our politicians look good. In the glare of the media, we went to extraordinary lengths to present them at their best, and they could be touchingly naive about our efforts, as an episode involving Tessa Jowell showed.

It was the 2001 general election and I was heading up the campaign operation at HQ. It was a great job and I really enjoyed it. In the last week of the campaign the polls were still tight and though we had a slim lead we were acutely aware we could not afford to be complacent. We needed the public to know we were fighting for every vote.

Some bright spark came up with the idea of campaigning at motorway service stations, to show we were so determined not to take votes for granted that we had ministers campaigning on the way to and from their higher-profile appearances. I thought the idea was crap, but I was wrong. We arranged for several ministers to be at service stations at set times and offered the media pictures, and everyone seemed enthusiastic. The main photo opportunities were at Fleet services on the M3, and we arranged for Tessa to call in on the way back to London from a campaign event in south Dorset.

Leaving nothing to chance, my team contacted the local Labour Party and arranged for thirty members to get to the northbound service station half an hour before Tessa arrived. Our trusty volunteers spread themselves out, bought coffee and waited, doing their best to look like ordinary punters having a breather from a long car journey. Tessa arrived on cue with TV crews, bought a coffee and chatted to folk who 'happened' to be at the service station. The pictures looked great and we got the story we wanted, that we were fighting tooth and nail for every vote.

Despite her status as New Labour royalty, Tessa was always grateful for the efforts of those lower down the pecking order, and had none of the airs and graces of some Cabinet colleagues. After the trip she went out of her way to come into Victoria Street and thank me and the team personally for the smooth organisation of the motorway visit. She confided that she had initially been sceptical about the stunt, but had been pleasantly surprised by how friendly the customers at the service station were. She said the warmth of her reception had convinced her we were going to win.

I simply didn't have the heart to tell her there was no way we let a senior minister walk into a service station in the glare of the media and meet random members of the public.

By then I was a very experienced operator, but my career in political campaigning had an inauspicious start. It was a few months before the 1997 general election and I had just started my first job for the party. My remit was to win the constituency of Battersea for Labour's candidate, Martin Linton. The problem for me was that while I was undoubtedly enthusiastic, committed and up for the fight, I had told a very slight white lie at my interview. Not unreasonably, I had been asked if I was computer literate, and my answer had been 'yes'. Strictly speaking this was not true. My career until then had been in nursing, and I barely knew where to find the power button on a computer. When I turned up for my first day at work in September 1996 my first challenge was working out how to turn on the machine; my second challenge was to become as computer literate as I had claimed without anyone noticing my incompetence. This was particularly problematic, since central to fighting and winning that particular general election campaign was exploiting the targeting capability of an alarmingly sophisticated piece of software called Elpack. I had read the manual – but not much else.

Somehow I muddled through and in a few weeks I built a fantastic team of campaigning volunteers determined to win Battersea for Labour at all costs. It was one of the happiest times of my life as I built a new circle of friends all dedicated to getting Martin into Westminster. There were many late nights, there was a lot of drinking, and we were all convinced we were running the best campaign in the country. It wasn't about policies, over which we often disagreed. Nor was it about the candidate. Much as we loved Martin it could have been anyone. It was tribal – Labour versus the Tories – and though Battersea was a long shot, we were going to fight to win, and we were going to do it as a team.

It's hard to explain to those who have never fought an election campaign the fierce loyalty that develops among staff and volunteers. Together we raised money, delivered hundreds of thousands of leaflets and knocked on countless doors. We printed direct mail, hand-wrote letters, and attended countless fundraising coffee mornings. We became friends, loyal to each other first and to our shared cause second. I know that the friendships I made during the 1997 campaign will be some of the most enduring of my life.

It was during that campaign that I began to learn the art of making politicians look good. If we could make our opponents look bad at the same time then so much the better. Two weeks before polling day I heard Virginia Bottomley was heading for Battersea in her 'battle bus' to campaign for the incumbent Tory MP, John Bowis. She was going to Battersea Arts Centre to promote some extra funding the Conservative government had given the facility and Bowis was due to meet her there. What the Tories had forgotten was that our candidate Martin was the chair of the Arts Centre, creating a delicious opportunity for mischief.

Bottomley was due at 10 a.m. so I did a quick ring round of volunteers and arranged for thirty Labour activists, complete with prominent red rosettes, to be drinking coffee in the Arts Centre café when she arrived. Martin demanded, and got, the right to be in the welcoming party. The battle bus rolled up, resplendent in pale blue livery with 'Ginny's Battle Bus' in large lettering down each side. It parked illegally at a bus stop and the minister and her entourage swept out. Someone alerted a traffic warden and the bus got a parking ticket, and the same 'someone' alerted the press just in case they missed it. The Labour supporters outnumbered the surprised handful of local Tories and Martin Linton, Labour candidate, was in every camera shot looking calm and collected, in contrast to a hassled Bottomley. That evening the *Evening Standard* ran a story about the visit under the headline 'Ginny's Campaign Visit From Hell' and as far as I was concerned it was one point to us, *nul points* to them.

On polling night I walked to the count at Wandsworth Town Hall ready for the worst. Months of campaigning, teamwork and effort came down to the next few hours. I was convinced that we had lost. The shock when we discovered our effort had paid off took some time to sink in. Of course as far as we were concerned, it wasn't a national swing, an unpopular Tory government or a dynamic Tony Blair that won it for us. No, we had won it for ourselves, Labour's team in Battersea.

Two subsequent general elections, two Scottish elections, two Welsh elections, three European elections, eleven by-elections and countless local elections later and the same principle was still true: campaigning was a team game focused on making our candidate, our politicians and our party look good, and if we could make the others look bad at the same time then so much the better.

Following the high of Labour's landslide victory in 1997, my contract in Battersea ended and I wasn't sure what I was going to do next. I briefly contemplated going back to nursing, but my heart wasn't in it. By now I was addicted to political campaigning, and I was thrilled when I managed to secure a temporary extension to my contract. A few weeks later, an attractive part-time administrator called Vilma Bermudez, who was studying law, joined the Battersea team. She was recently single and had a three-year-old daughter called Ivanna. It wasn't all plain sailing but six years later we were married and Ivanna was my daughter in all but name.

In the meantime I had fought the 1998 local elections in Wandsworth and told everyone who would listen that Labour was going to win. In fact we were hammered by the Tories, and for the first time, I learned what it was like to lose. I suppose I had begun to take victory in campaigns for granted and it was a big shock to be brought back down to size.

By the 1999 European elections I was employed at Head Office and had spent a year working in the party's election unit. My post was elections officer and I considered myself a bit of a pro. At the very least my job title now indicated expertise, and I couldn't believe that I was still being paid to do something that a few years earlier I had been doing as a hobby. Even wandering the streets of London with a colleague who was dressed as a sardine didn't dampen my enthusiasm. It was the inaugural London mayoral election and the sardine stunt was designed to highlight the alleged impact of Ken Livingstone's transport policies on London commuters. Sadly the stunt failed and the campaign as a whole was a disaster: Ken, who had run as an independent, walked into office with Labour's Frank Dobson trailing in third. Frank was a good man and deserved better. Ironically, three years later Ken was back in the party.

As the 2001 general election approached, I was seconded to manage Labour's campaign in the East of England. It was a promotion and I was very excited, even though it meant moving to a hotel in Ipswich at twenty-four hours' notice. I told Vilma it would only be for a few weeks, but unfortunately the election was delayed due to the foot-and-mouth outbreak and, what with one thing and another, six months later I was still there. Eventually, in October 2001 the position became permanent and Vilma and Ivanna moved east and joined me.

As campaign manager my main job once the election was called was to organise high-profile visits to the area by senior Labour figures. It was a huge logistical operation involving up to three different visit programmes per day in different parts of the region. Unfortunately, ministers seemed to expect the same levels of service from the party machine as they enjoyed from the government outside election times. The reality was that the smooth running of this machine depended on a handful of overstretched staff, hundreds of volunteers and a lot of luck. We lived in constant fear of being responsible for a PR disaster.

Crucial to the success of visits was ensuring we never let the visiting ministers out of our sight. Their reputation was in our hands, and they would look us for reassurance, instruction and next steps. It meant they could appear relaxed, knowing that someone was watching their back and would let them know when to move on and where to go next.

Losing a politician meant you could no longer provide the reassurance and logistics they needed. It was not a situation that enhanced the career of either the politician or the visit organiser.

The 2001 election campaign started to warm up when Robin Cook got his car egged in Norwich. It got warmer still when, luckily with no one noticing, John Prescott nearly had a scuffle with a protestor in Bedford. He got off his 'Prescott Express' coach in a bad mood, and his temper was not improved when towards the end of his soapbox speech someone in the crowd became mouthy. Before we knew it people began pushing and shoving, and it looked like he might be caught up in an embarrassing fracas. Luckily his team managed to extract him from the fray and manoeuvre him back to his coach before anything serious kicked off, but it was a sobering moment. Of course a few weeks later JP went one stage further and actually punched someone when he was on a visit to Wales. Sadly on that occasion it was in full view of the press.

It was bad enough organising visits to the region by Cabinet ministers but visits by the Prime Minister were a whole different ball game. The party would put in place a massive team of people to support the carnival that accompanies the leader, and nothing whatsoever was left to chance. At any one time there was a team at Head Office responsible for logistics, policy research and media, while on the road there was a team of up to fifteen people with the leader, plus security and a coachful of journalists – all of whom had paid for the privilege of being there. In addition there would be four advance teams at HQ working on future visits.

Wherever the leader travelled he was under intense scrutiny, and we knew that even the tiniest error in choreography would be pounced on by a media pack desperate for bad news. It was vital to prevent any unscheduled contact between the Prime Minister and members of the public. Everything possible was done to minimise the chance of mistakes but things could still go wrong, and during Tony's first foray into the East of England in the 2001 election they certainly did.

The plan was simple enough: first a visit to the newly refurbished Queen Elizabeth Hospital in King's Lynn, with a quick tour of the premises and in particular a look at the children's centre; then on to a small village in deepest, darkest rural Tory Norfolk to knock on the doors of some known Labour voters. Finally, he would hold a question-and-answer session at the University of East Anglia. It should have been easy. Two days before the big visit we had a run through and it all looked good. The rural Labour supporters were all in a small cul-de-sac that also contained a Labour-friendly GP surgery and we had 'vote Labour' posters in virtually every garden. The pictures were going to be great: a relaxed Tony wandering down a leafy garden path, a knock at the door, and hey presto! a happy Labour (rural) voter would emerge. The Q&A was with an invited audience and we were confident it would be a breeze.

Accompanied by Cherie, Tony was due at the hospital at 10 a.m. I was up at five so that I could drive from Ipswich and be in place a couple of hours before his arrival. Such visits involved checking everything and then checking it again, so it was always wise to leave plenty of time.

En route to the hospital I got a call from one of the PM's team asking if I could make sure that there were half a dozen 'obviously sick' children for Tony to meet. It was 6.45 a.m., I was halfway to King's Lynn, and I was already knackered and stressed. An additional mission to find 'obviously sick' children was not part of the game plan. The result was that I spent several hours scouring hospital wards for poorly-looking kids, trying to be sensitive and diplomatic about it, all the while aware that the clock was ticking. Finally we found the requisite children, obtained permission from their parents for them to take part and had them in position about thirty seconds before Tony turned up with fifty bored journalists.

The eleventh-hour instruction meant that we ran out of time to check Tony's route through the hospital, so we had to run ahead of his party on each phase of the tour to ensure there were no dangers lurking. At one stage I realised that Cherie was no longer with us. Trying not to panic I sent someone back the way we had come and they found her chatting to a member of the public, a dangerous habit in a hospital. There was simply too much risk of a PR disaster involving some patient or relative unhappy with the NHS.

In the original visit plan the regional campaign team had been due to leave the hospital twenty minutes before Tony, while he was meeting (obviously sick) children. This was to allow us time to arrive in the village well in advance for the next stage of the visit, with Tony's convoy deliberately taking its time to arrive. We could then hook up with the team already in place in the cul-de-sac, check all was well and calmly wait for his arrival, when we would cheer like mad. But the delays at the hospital threw our carefully laid exit plans into chaos, with the result that Tony's convoy left before we did. The police held up traffic and he ended up with a fifteen-minute head start.

I wasn't unduly worried, thinking we could always call the convoy and tell them to slow down, let us past or 'drive around the block'. Excited at being part of the programme, the driver of the car I was travelling in put his foot down and stayed steadily over the speed limit. I reached for my mobile to tell Tony's convoy to pull back, but there was no signal. It was a disaster waiting to happen: I couldn't find out what was going on in the cul-de-sac and couldn't communicate with Tony's convoy. At one point we caught up with the convoy and considered overtaking. However, we thought better of it, since the convoy consisted of about ten vehicles and a lot of armed protection staff. We couldn't let them know who we were and even for me, getting shot while trying to make sure Tony looked good seemed a bit extreme. So Tony arrived at the cul-de-sac before we did and the police wouldn't let us park when we got there. By the time we'd found somewhere to leave the car and run back he'd been there for ten minutes and I hadn't a clue what was going on.

Despite our efforts to keep the visit under wraps, somehow news had spread and several hundred pro-hunting demonstrators had descended. When Tony was driven in to the cul-de-sac, they barricaded him in and by the time we arrived they were screaming abuse. Around twenty doughty Labour supporters were doing their best to level things up, but they were no match for the throng. The police were very nervous and wouldn't let us into the cul-de-sac and even my very best 'Don't you know who I am?' routine cut no ice.

After a twenty-minute stand-off the police decided enough was enough and extracted Tony from the mêlée. He was whisked off to Norwich for the Q&A. I tried phoning the convoy to apologise for what had happened but my phone still wasn't working. I correctly assumed the pictures would be terrible.

Consoling myself that there was still the Q&A to end the day on a positive note, we headed off to the university. Everyone was calm, the guests were arriving, the set was built and it all looked good. What could go wrong? Sadly I had failed to account for the police, who had omitted to provide any security barriers. There was only one very narrow approach road to the campus, and with just an hour to go before Tony's arrival, around 100 protestors rolled up and lined the road. I couldn't bear it – three hours earlier I had managed to get Tony lost in a cul-de-sac and now it seemed I was going to get him shut out of the Q&A. After much negotiation with the police and some carefully organised counter-demonstrations that distracted the protestors, we got Tony in. An hour late the Q&A started and so did the rain, which flushed out the protestors so that at least Tony's departure was a little more relaxed.

That evening over a beer and curry with a colleague there wasn't much to cheer. All we could do was comfort ourselves that they wouldn't send Tony back to the East of England region again before polling day.

But we were wrong. Someone at Head Office decided that the campaign felt staged and wanted Tony and Cherie to be seen talking to 'real people'. During the penultimate week of the campaign, I received a phone call to say Tony was going to go to Basildon and they wanted him to be seen relaxing and chatting with locals. Cherie would be with him.

The next day I went to do a recce in Basildon with the advance team and met Angela Smith, the incumbent Labour candidate. After considering a few options we settled on a visit to the Vange & Pitsea Working Men's Club, which seemed spacious and unlikely to become overly crowded, and which had a friendly atmosphere. All we said was that we were bringing a senior politician and the visit was due to take place at 3 p.m. the next day – Friday. On Friday morning we had a team out knocking on local doors inviting friendly Labour voters to come and meet a senior Labour figure at the club. Though we should have known better, we assumed it would all be straightforward. The fifty or so media would arrive first and would be kept penned in around the edges of the room, while drinkers (most of whom would be our invited friendlies) would be sitting in the club. The idea was that Tony and Cherie would circulate freely accompanied by me, talk to a few people, then leave.

Our guests had been asked to arrive at 2.30 p.m. but, as it was a Friday, the club was heaving by 2.00. By the time the extras appeared there was standing room only. The media arrived, the temperature and atmosphere rose and the drink was flowing freely. Just after three Tony and Cherie arrived. There was a great moment when the club steward insisted on signing them both in and giving them temporary memberships. Tony loved it. I accompanied them in to the club. The plan was to walk them slowly to the bar, shaking hands as we went along. At the bar, they would buy a drink and chat before walking slowly out shaking more hands. Of course it would all be in the full glare of the live TV feeds and countless snappers. The room was so busy that even the personal protection team who never left Tony's side couldn't follow, so it was just me.

For the first couple of tables all went smoothly. People were chatting and Tony and Cherie were great. My job was diplomatically to move them on after a polite period of chat and stay out of the camera shots. Suddenly Cherie decided to sit down at a table and someone went to get her a drink, while Tony headed off towards the bar. I was not sure who I should abandon – Cherie or Tony? Either was a big risk. I headed for the bar and was relieved to see that people were being friendly. Then just over Tony's shoulder, I saw a bare-chested bald man with an awful lot of tattoos looking agitated and heading our way. He was bigger than Tony, definitely bigger than me, and the protection people were some distance away. He was pushing people out of the way to get to Tony, beer was being spilled, and he raised his hand. I knew that if it came to throwing myself in the way of his fist I couldn't do it.

'Oi, Tony!' he shouted live on TV. I held my breath. Tony smiled. 'Good on you mate, good on you!' he said. He thrust his hand out to the PM and shook vigorously. I breathed a sigh of relief – for an awful moment it had really looked like Tony was going to get punched and none of his protection team would have been there to intervene.

No time to relax, though – where was Cherie? We needed to make our way out of the club slowly, and I asked Tony to stay put while I went to find her. I pushed my way through the thronging drinkers, trying to see through the crowd to the table where she'd been sitting when I left, but once again she'd disappeared. By the time I found her and quietly told her we needed to move, Tony had moved and I couldn't see him.

Cherie and I headed to where we thought he was and the cameras kept rolling. We found him surrounded by people with half a bitter in his hand, looking perfectly relaxed. We slowly moved out of the club and finally they left. I was so relieved to see the back of them. Still, despite the chaos and near miss with the tattooed heavy, the pictures were great and colleagues watching the live footage back at Head Office had a great laugh at the terrified expressions on my face as our carefully laid plans unravelled.

With hindsight the 2001 election was easy – we were always going to win. The 2005 election was very different. The Iraq War had poisoned the political atmosphere. In the previous two years, party offices around the country had been vandalised, someone threw paint at HQ, and we had even had staff taken hostage by anti-war protestors in our Bristol office. Conferences were nervous affairs where we expected to be infiltrated by protestors, and often were. The run-up to the start of the campaign was dominated by what we called Tony's 'masochism strategy', which saw him shouted at, insulted and slow-handclapped in very public ways at conferences and in TV studios across the country. The view was that he needed to face his critics head on.

It was in this environment that we planned a general election with the tightest opinion polls since 1992, when we had lost. Nerves were jangling and the relationship between Tony and Gordon was frayed. Each had their own pollsters and strategists as they didn't trust the other's, all paid for by the party. It was a farcical situation, with the Chancellor and his acolytes seemingly more concerned about outdoing the Prime Minister than winning over voters. Internally, the campaign was dominated by the bolstering of each camp with increasing numbers of advisers and experts. Party staff looked on with incredulity as yet another wonk joined Labour's team. We all knew that in reality, they had joined to beef up either Tony or Gordon's crew.

On the whole, the Treasury team was frugal. The same could not be said for the leader's team. There was a hierarchy: established party staff had budgets and discipline, but the leader's team, comprising No. 10

staff and a large number of drafted-in 'volunteers,' expected a state-of-the-art mobile phone, expense accounts and preferential treatment. While staff from HQ were avoiding booking taxis to keep costs low, the leader's team were charging everything to hotel tabs. Watching from the fringes it was an unedifying spectacle: we looked drunk on the trappings of power. I hated it.

The low point was a 'Make Poverty History' rally at the Old Vic theatre. It was a 'celebration' of our achievements in alleviating third world poverty, something we were rightly proud of. Unfortunately the event, with a live satellite link-up to poor people in Africa and President Clinton in the United States, cost hundreds of thousands of pounds to stage. It was the ultimate vanity exercise which attracted virtually no media coverage, and I was ashamed.

My job was to head up the key campaign operation, the national version of the job I had undertaken in the East of England in 2001. For the last day of the campaign, we had planned what we hoped would be a spectacular photo opportunity. The idea was that after the final press conference was over, a select group of ministers would be whisked off in helicopters for a final campaign blitz. There were six helicopters in total, a real *Apocalypse Now* moment that cost the cash-strapped party thousands of pounds. Naively, we assumed we would have a queue of ministers wanting to take part, but they had been in power too long to be excited by such gigs. We kept asking but ministers were only prepared to do it if they could be dropped off home by helicopter at the end of the visit programme. At one point we were in serious danger of having ministerless helicopters.

After the polls closed, a small team gathered in Victoria Street to process all the intelligence from polling stations and counts around the country. While the rest of the staff headed to the National Portrait Gallery for the start of the polling night celebrations we hungrily collated results. Our psephologist, Greg Cook, monitored and analysed information as it rolled in. What started on a high – we expected to win – rapidly became quite fraught as victory looked less assured. Up in Sedgefield Tony was worried and his flight from the north-east to London was delayed in case we had lost or there was a hung parliament. Finally, in the early hours it became clear that we had been returned to power with a decent majority and Tony's flight was able to leave. Relieved, we all walked up Whitehall to the NPG and joined a well-established party waiting for a victorious Tony's arrival.

Less than a year later I was General Secretary and the climate was even more challenging. We were heading for a very difficult set of local elections with a young and dynamic new Tory leader facing his first electoral test. The Prime Minister was under pressure to announce a departure date and behind the scenes Gordon was aggressively pushing a 'Tony has to go' line. 'Cash for honours' was raging and money was tight. It was my first national electoral challenge since I'd got the top job.

It was always a struggle to engage the public in local election campaigns, so we invented a character called 'Dave the Chameleon' to liven things up. This animated little reptile was our tongue-in-cheek way of gently poking fun at the new Tory leader, who was popular with the public but something of an unknown quantity. We knew it would be difficult for us to land a punch and wanted to find a lighthearted way of portraying him as willing to say or do anything to win votes. It was a personal attack but we hoped it was gentle enough for us to get away with it. It was something of a morale booster for us, a way to make us feel we were fighting back when in truth, less than a year after a third general electoral victory, we were feeling battered. Philip Gould and Ben Wegg-Prosser loved the whole concept and so did I. Though Tony, JP and Gordon were all unsure whether it would work, we had some great creative minds working on the campaign and everybody at HQ was excited. It was light relief from the travails of 'cash for honours'.

Dave the Chameleon's first public outing was an election broadcast early in the campaign. We had a pre-launch at Victoria Street during which we distributed T-shirts and mugs to the press. The journalists loved it and the media coverage was excellent. We were inundated with phone and email responses when the election broadcast went out, the majority positive. Thousands of people downloaded Dave ringtones or screen savers, and it was our most viewed, interacted and enjoyed broadcast in recent years.

Buoyed by the response, we went into overdrive, planning an

amazing second episode with journalists getting Dave the Chameleon sweets, a live webcam of a real living chameleon and a life-size Dave cycling down Victoria Street. We were sure it would get everybody talking. However, just as we were about to launch the next phase, with staff working eighteen-hour days to prepare, a scandal broke in the media about foreign prisoners in British jails being released into the community after serving their sentences instead of being deported. The TV bulletins and newspapers were full of stories about muggers and rapists, all the government's fault. Suddenly our humorous broadcast about Dave didn't seem appropriate.

The day before it was due to be aired the election team had an 8.30 a.m. meeting at Victoria Street and discussed what to do. Ian McCartney insisted that we abandon the extra stunts associated with the broadcast. I was gutted as we'd worked so hard on the plans, and I couldn't wait to see our bloke in his chameleon costume cycling down the street. I argued that too much effort had gone in to cancel the project now, and Ian and I had really sharp words. He was unnecessarily rude but he was right. If we'd pressed ahead we would have looked flippant and it would have backfired. The second Dave broadcast was screened without the stunts.

So Dave the Chameleon died a death. He was nothing without the creative drive and political buy-in of our senior politicians. In any case, voters seemed to think he was really cute, which was not exactly the effect we were hoping for. Indeed, the Tory leader liked his alter ego so much he put a sticker of Dave on his fridge door. Would the chameleon have lived to fight another day had it not been for the release of foreign prisoners? Who knows, but he was fun while he lasted.

# 7. MONEY, MONEY, MONEY

## A RICH MAN'S WORLD

It was that heady time after winning the 2005 general election, when the long summer days stretched ahead and Labour staff could put their feet up and bask in the glory of a successful campaign. Everyone except me seemed to be having fun. In the office, the talk was all of who was going on holiday where, and the air buzzed with happy banter about how people were planning to spend their election bonuses.

I was also thinking about money: in fact, I was thinking about nothing else.

I had just started my new role as Labour's director of finance, a job I had never wanted and would probably have run a mile from accepting had I known what it would entail. Only a few days after taking up the post, I began to realise what I had let myself in for. I felt so overwhelmed by the party's mountain of debt and the burden that was now on my shoulders that I actually shed tears.

'I don't think I can do it,' I whimpered feebly to Vilma. 'I don't think this is how I want to live my life.'

We were sitting in our back garden, me with my head in my hands, despairing over the enormity of the task I faced. I felt completely out of my depth, and really resentful to have found myself in this position. Matt, who'd appointed me, seemed oblivious to the scale of the problem. We had millions of pounds worth of election bills which had to be settled within three weeks or we'd be breaking the law. The amount outstanding was something like £8 million. I also had to find about £1.4 million to pay the staff that month. Our credit cards were maxed out and we had hit our overdraft limit. We had some very modest reserves, but nowhere near enough to cover the staff wage bill. Just what was I missing here? How could Matt be so relaxed?

I had only just started the job, but for the first time in my life, I was really experiencing the physical effects of stress. I could not sleep.

'Get a grip,' Vilma told me sternly. 'You'll be fine. You'll soon find your feet.'

I went back to work the next day with renewed determination. I could have cried with relief when a few days later, gifts totalling £1 million arrived out of the blue. Suddenly the pressure was off. I could pay the staff and even some of the bills. For the first time since I'd started the job, I felt relaxed enough to take a lunch break. I wandered out to a local delicatessen and bought a really nice fresh cheese and pickle sandwich. As I was heading along the street, clutching the roll in its paper bag, my mobile rang. It was our bank, the Co-operative. 'I see you've got some money in,' the guy from the bank observed.

'Yes, it's great news, isn't it?' I replied happily, looking forward to my sandwich.

'Yeah, we've just taken it off you,' he shot back. 'We're not sure you're going to get much else in soon, so you can't draw on it.'

There was a moment of stunned silence as I absorbed this news.

'How am I going to pay the staff?' I squeaked – but it was not his problem. Feeling sick, I chucked the cheese sandwich into a litter bin. I remember almost laughing in disbelief. 'This could be the shortest time anyone has ever spent as finance director,' I thought grimly. I could not see myself lasting for more than another week if this was what it was going to be like.

By the time I got back to the office, I'd calmed down a bit. I sat down at my desk, and called the Co-op guy back, requesting a teleconference that afternoon with his boss. Then I went to see Matt. 'I can't pay the staff,' I said. Their salaries were due in four days.

'It'll be all right,' he shrugged.

His attitude wound me up. I suppose he'd seen it all before, and in the past, things had always worked out in the end, but the reality was that a solution was not just going to appear out of the ether. I had to make it happen.

During the teleconference with the Co-op, I had the clear impression I was being tested. They knew I did not have a financial background, and that cannot have instilled confidence. So they put me through my paces, seeing if I could argue my case.

'If you take all that money off me, I won't be able to pay the staff. Then we'll have a very public crisis,' I told them as calmly as I could. 'That will jeopardise our other funding, and the situation will escalate. So here's what I suggest as a compromise – you leave me enough money from the £1 million donation income to ensure that I can pay them, and take the rest.'

They grudgingly agreed and for a brief interlude the heat was off. I had no idea that what I'd just endured was a typical week.

In my new job, I soon discovered that few people who worked for the party cared where the money came from. They were quite happy to spend it, but never stopped to think of the consequences of running up huge debts. As far as they were concerned, it was someone else's problem. The reality was that between 1996 and 2006 there was only one year that the party brought in more than it spent. Year after year, we accumulated debt.

Before the landslide of 1997, the party had largely relied on funding from the trade unions but when Michael Levy became involved in fundraising in 1996, we began attracting high value donations from wealthy individuals. This money was supposed to be the icing on the cake, allowing us to compete with the Tories, billboard for billboard, poster for poster, in the election campaign, but soon such gifts became an integral part of our budget. As budgets were prepared for the year ahead each autumn, the party would decide what it was going to spend, calculate how much could be expected from the unions and membership subscriptions, and Michael would be asked to find the difference. He would go off and prepare a schedule of donors and let us know how much they said they could give.

The problem was that the system relied on donors doing exactly what they said they would do, exactly when they said they would do it. Increasingly, we depended on a relatively small number of very rich individuals, who generously wrote us large cheques. But we had no control at all. Just getting hold of these people was a nightmare. They were international businessmen, who were often abroad in different time zones, and they were always busy. As you'd expect, they employed staff to keep beggars off their backs. We had no choice but to dance to their tune, so if they said they could only speak to us at 4 a.m. UK time, that's when I would have to pick up the phone. I remember on one occasion, during the leader's speech at party conference, standing at the back of the hall frantically trying to have a conversation with a donor in the States on a crackly line. Tony's voice was booming out in the background and I could hardly hear, but I needed to persuade the man to bring forward a gift he had pledged and it was the only time he could talk. I could not be seen to leave the hall during Tony's speech.

Yet we were always pissing money away. I discovered soon after I became finance director that the finance team did not make a habit of talking to the people in the party who spent the money. Staff in roles that involved buying or commissioning things, whether billboard space or new photocopiers, purchased whatever they wanted or needed virtually without consulting anyone. There was a casual assumption that the money would somehow be found. The finance team kept a stack of cheques in a filing cabinet and would pull them out to pay bills whenever there was enough money in the bank. It was no way to run a business.

The farcical extent to which our fate rested in the hands of a few multi-millionaires was highlighted on 7 July 2005, the day of the London bombings. That day, I was supposed to be picking up a cheque for £2 million from Lakshmi Mittal, the steel tycoon, who was a long-standing financial backer of the party. The banks were desperate for the money but quite reasonably Lakshmi wanted to control exactly when he handed it over. Michael and I had spent a long time gently trying to encourage him to get it to us as soon as possible.

Eventually he agreed to give me a post-dated cheque, which we could photocopy and show the banks to keep them off our backs. I got a call from his office on 6 July saying he would give it to us the following day.

I was due to catch a train early the following morning to visit our Newcastle office, but we were so desperate for the cash I could not risk the cheque going astray. So I postponed my trip, arranging to pick up the cheque in person first thing in the morning. I figured I could head up to Newcastle as soon as I had the cheque in my hands and bank it there.

I arrived at Waterloo station just as they were closing the Tube. The first bombs had just gone off. Oblivious to the crisis, I jumped into a cab and headed over to Lakshmi's office. By now there was pandemonium in London, as huge areas had been sealed off by the police. The city screamed with the wail of sirens and all mobile networks went down, but I was entirely focused on getting that cheque in my pocket. Lakshmi was as good as his word, and I was able to pick it up without further difficulty, but it was obvious there was no way I was going to get up to Newcastle that day. King's Cross was closed and it would have been ridiculous to have even attempted the journey. I walked back to the office, completely preoccupied by the party's cashflow problems. As I hurried into HQ I noticed a brand new rucksack full of stuff lying at the bottom of the stairs.

I eyed it warily, and rang the receptionist.

'Fuck me!' she shouted, and dialled 999. The police said we should evacuate the building immediately, so I ran from floor to floor, leading everyone out of the building – straight past the suspect rucksack. In my attempt to be the hero I had forgotten that we had a back door. We all hung around outside for about an hour before the police arrived and blew it up. It turned out to have been stolen from a tourist and didn't contain anything of interest, but we were always a potential target, and on a day when bombs were going off at Underground stations and a bus had been blown up, there was no way anyone was taking any chances.

It was about 4.45 p.m. when we finally trooped back into the office, and at last I was able to get through to the bank and explain why they hadn't received their photocopy of the cheque. Only then did I think to phone Vilma, who went absolutely nuts, because I hadn't contacted her all day. She knew I had been planning to go to King's Cross that morning, and she had not been able to track me down. She had spent the whole day panicking that I'd been hurt or killed. I was so obsessed with my mission that I hadn't actually occurred to me to call her.

The next day, I went into the office wearing a different suit. When I arrived I realised I'd left the cheque in the pocket of the outfit I'd worn the day before. It was hanging in the wardrobe. After all that, I couldn't even bank the bloody thing. I spent much of the day having irrational visions of the kids scribbling on it or putting it in the washing machine.

This is what the job was like week in, week out, as we lurched from one financial crisis to the next, hopelessly hand to mouth. On one occasion the banks messed up the BACS transfer system we used to pay everyone, and staff did not get their salaries on the morning they were due. They all thought we'd literally run out of money and who could blame them? It was closer to being true than they knew. I was really worried that there would be a public panic and organised one of those 'telephone tree' systems to make sure everyone got a call reassuring them it was just a technical glitch.

Right from the start, it was obvious to me that we had to cut jobs. However, Matt would not hear of it. He would say things like, 'You can make redundancies when you are General Secretary, but it's not going to happen on my watch.' My hands were tied until he left. In any case, during my short stint as finance director before I took over as General Secretary, I kept thinking I must be missing something. I was a financial virgin and I could not believe the situation was as chaotic as it seemed.

That autumn, I asked the party's accountant to give me a budget forecast for 2006. It was quite clear from the document he produced that our situation was unsustainable. 'Unless we bring in £8 million in donations, on top of what we'll get from the trade unions, we'll have to cut staff and other things,' he said bluntly.

I went and told Matt.

'Go and check the figures,' he instructed. 'They can't be right.'

It was clear I was on my own with this one. Our monthly staff bill, for 360 employees, was over £1 million, and it had to be paid on the twentieth. I spent my entire time ducking and diving to make ends meet. Roughly speaking, we needed a £2½ million monthly income just to cover our costs. Some months we would find ourselves £½ million short; other months it was a bit easier, but we were always desperately scratching around.

Matt left at the end of December 2005 and I was finally free to do what I knew had to be done. I resented starting my new role as General Secretary like this. Matt had not even allowed me to warn people that job cuts were unavoidable. Previous General Secretaries had swept in and done popular things like buying funky new furniture, and I had come in and started axing jobs. It was a poor introduction to my regime, but there was no choice. We began with a voluntary redundancy scheme.

I called staff across the country together for a meeting and was honest about the situation. I agreed a new budget with the banks which forced us to operate within our means. Any surplus would be siphoned off to reduce our debt. In addition to the money we owed the banks, we had loans to repay. It was another source of anxiety but not the most pressing issue at this stage. I was quietly confident that our private lenders, all of whom were supporters of the party, would be flexible about repayment terms, and hoped at least some could eventually be persuaded to convert their loans into donations.

In a sense, as 2005 rolled into 2006, things weren't looking too bad. Thanks to Michael, we were expecting between £4 million and £5 million to come in during the year, and the banks could see we had a plan in place to cut costs. The situation was very delicate but felt a bit more stable than usual. For the first time since taking charge of the party's finances, I was beginning to feel a bit more in control.

## BANKRUPTCY BECKONS

I had been General Secretary for three months when the 'cash for honours' scandal erupted. Overnight, our income dried up. Now more than ever we needed our banks, the Co-operative and Unity Trust, to remain on side.

I remember the first meeting with them after the police announced they were investigating allegations of the sale of peerages. By now, I knew the people who handled our account well. There were three executives from the Co-op with whom I dealt regularly, and one guy from Unity.

We meet in the board room in Victoria Street, and I rolled out the red carpet, by which I mean I wheeled out the cafetière and even laid on some Jaffa Cakes. We had banned biscuits at HQ as an unnecessary luxury so this was pretty special treatment. I remember making some flippant comment about how the 'cash for honours' scandal might delay the £4½ million we were expecting to come in 'by a few weeks'. 'It's a storm in a tea cup. We'll ride it out. There's no danger of any of the loans being called in and we're talking to the lenders,' I told them cheerfully.

They thanked me for my candour; there was a bit of small talk about cricket, and then they left. Looking back I'm embarrassed at how glib I was. How wrong could I be? Perhaps it's a good thing I didn't know what lay ahead.

From about April until July, when Michael was arrested, Roy Kennedy and I would talk to the banks every fortnight. The conversations were always the same: I would reassure them that we were stripping back costs and update them on the voluntary redundancy scheme, which was going well. They would seek reassurances that the lenders were not demanding repayment and that we remained confident of income. They often wanted to discuss the detail of risky areas of business like our annual conference, where we could either make a little bit or lose a lot depending on how smart we were.

It was a sad time, as colleagues I'd known for years took the decision to leave. We were doing everything we could to cut costs. There was a ban on travel by taxi, and whenever I went out my PA would print me off a street map so I could use public transport. I would dutifully put it in my pocket then jump in a cab anyway and just pay the fare myself. I supposed I'd got used to such luxuries. We became much more efficient as an organisation and though membership of the party was falling, we were making more money from each person so our revenue actually rose a little.

However, there was still no sign of the £4½ million, and we were running out of time.

Every June, political parties must file their annual accounts, and we had to prove that we were still a 'going concern'. The accounts were not simply a record of the preceding year, they were also the forum for independent auditors to verify the party was financially sound enough to continue trading for another twelve months. This was necessary to reassure everyone with whom we did business that we could pay the bills. If we could not secure this vote of confidence from the auditors, we would have to cease trading.

The looming deadline was a huge source of anxiety. Over recent years our accounts had shown rising levels of debt. However, at the time there had been no obvious danger of any of our debt being called in, and in any case, donations were still flowing into the party. Now the political landscape was very different. For the first time there was a real risk one or more of the lenders would suddenly demand repayment, and we had almost nothing coming in. In order to sign us off as a going concern for the next twelve months, the auditors needed to be sure that none of our loans, either from supporters or from the banks, would be called in.

Some of the loans were not due to be repaid until 2007 or 2008 anyway, but there was a question mark over around £7 million. We needed every single one of the lenders to tell us their intention, and I spent about three weeks in tense negotiation with all of those involved. Often their gatekeepers would not allow me to talk to them directly, and I was forced to relay increasingly desperate messages through middlemen. I had not dealt with all these individuals personally before, and really missed Michael's input. Amid the police inquiry, he was not keen to be involved.

One by one, we began picking the lenders off, securing the guarantees we needed that they would not demand repayment for at least another year. However, uncertainty remained over £3 million, the lenders in these cases refusing to give us any promise. I tried a new tactic, ringing round other financial supporters asking if they could act as guarantors if any of those lenders suddenly wanted their money back. A few people agreed and at last it looked like we were covered. I remember sitting on a train up to Newcastle, thinking we'd finally sorted everything out, then getting a phone call to say one of the guarantors had changed his mind. There were so many false dawns.

In desperation, I went to see David Sainsbury, who had always been good to the party, and appealed for his help. He said he would love to, but because of 'cash for honours' didn't feel able this time. It was the same old refrain – nobody wanted to be seen giving us money in such a toxic climate. There were only two days go before the accounts had to be filed.

Downing Street was fully aware of the impending disaster. I had spoken to David Hill and Ruth Turner explaining the full implications of failing to get the accounts signed off and they had informed Tony. I also informed the NEC officers, who were vaguely sympathetic, but their attitude seemed to be that it would all work itself out.

This pissed me off. 'It won't work *itself* out,' I thought. 'Obviously the only person who's going to sort it out is *me*.'

I felt deeply resentful that if the party went down the pan, it would forever be remembered as having been on my watch. Other General Secretaries had led the party to greatness and glory; yet here I was, through little fault of my own, about to lead the party to bankruptcy. The injustice of it ate away at me. It's easy to manage an organisation when it's on the way up, but a totally different story managing it when it's on the skids.

At about 4.30 p.m. the day before the accounts were due, gallows humour kicked in. 'This time tomorrow we won't even be able to go and buy a stamp. Let's use up all the credit on the franking machine,' Roy and I joked.

I couldn't really believe what was happening. Labour, the party of government, was about to go bankrupt, and hardly anyone knew. At 4.45 p.m., I decided to give it one last go on the phone with the two lenders who were digging in their heels. For the first time in weeks, I managed to get through to both of them directly. 'We are going to go bankrupt tomorrow, and if that happens, you will lose your money,' I said bluntly. I had nothing to lose, and I didn't want to leave them in any doubt about how high the stakes were now.

I pressed on. 'I know you're angry but we need to keep this organisation viable. You have been so good to us and we need your help more than ever now. Do you really want to be the one who pulls the plug on the Labour Party?'

In just over ten minutes, I had sorted it out – just like that! After weeks and weeks of anxiety and hopeless phone calls to gatekeepers, we were saved. I faxed the last remaining assurances straight through to the auditors and at 6 p.m. we received a call from them saying they were satisfied. I went to the loo and retched. Then Roy and I went to the pub and I got absolutely smashed. For the first half hour, the two of us could barely talk, we were so traumatised. But soon we were full of the usual bravado.

'Never in any doubt,' I grinned, swilling my beer.

'Never in any doubt,' Roy agreed.

'Bastards,' I said, referring pretty generally to everyone except us.

'Bastards,' Roy agreed, and we got another round in.

When I got home I had to sober up pretty quickly. The next day was the National Policy Forum at the ExCeL centre in Docklands and I needed to be on top of my game. Peering into the mirror in my slightly boozy state, I realised my hair was a mess. I had let myself go in all the stress of the previous weeks. Being vain, I didn't like the thought of everyone seeing me looking such a state, so I asked Vilma to cut it. It doesn't look so grey if it's short. We have some hair clippers that we use for the kids so she dug them out and set to work. It was late and she was tired, and she chose the wrong setting. After the first attempt, my hair was all clumpy.

'There's no choice. I'm going to have to go shorter,' she said, sounding worried. Afterwards I ran my hand over my head and felt a surge of panic.

'Give me the mirror!' I shouted. When I saw how I looked I practically started crying – this haircut it was so bad you could see my scalp through it.

'I can't believe this,' I moaned. 'I've got to stand up in front of hundreds of people tomorrow looking like a bloody squaddie.'

When I got to ExCeL on Friday, everyone immediately started taking the piss. I was pale, tired and almost bald. I couldn't help thinking that my dad, who was dying of cancer at the time, probably looked better than I did right then.

The next day, Tony was due at the ExCeL centre. Banks of TV cameras and photographers were assembled awaiting his arrival. I was tired, pissed off, and still had very short hair. Near the entrance to the conference centre was a huge flight of stairs, and when I heard Tony had arrived, I headed down to greet him. All the cameras were on us. Tony put on his trademark grin and wished the media scrum good morning, but through clenched teeth, he whispered, 'Oh my God, what have you done to your hair?' Then he patted my head – right there on live TV. Somewhere on the internet the footage of that excruciating moment still exists, me with a fixed smile as the Prime Minister brushes his hand over my scalp.

My public humiliation was not over. When Tony appeared on the stage to give his speech to the party, his opening line was: 'Hello everyone and welcome. I've just got to say, what on earth has Peter done to his hair?' Even I laughed.

Earlier, he'd taken me into a side room and thanked me for getting the accounts signed off. 'I know what a nightmare it's been. It must have been dreadful. So thanks, I really appreciate it,' he said.

I had not been expecting him to say anything about it and was grateful. It was a credit to him and Ruth, who had left him in no doubt about what I'd been through. Despite his confidence all along that it would 'all work out', I think he recognised that if we had gone bankrupt he would have had to quit.

Yet our money troubles were far from over. In July, Michael was arrested in the 'cash for honours' inquiry, completely severing our link to the wealthy donors on whom we depended. Though he had kept his distance from the party since the scandal broke, we had been hoping he would soon be able to resume his work. Ironically, we had just arranged for a big advert to appear in *The Times* featuring a list of our supporters and some blurb about how proud they were to be associated with the Labour Party. The message we were trying to get across was that it was still okay to give money to the party. Jack Dromey wasn't keen – I don't think he liked the idea of the party being so closely associated with the rich – and it felt a bit desperate, but we were trying to come up with ways to restore confidence and break the donation log jam. There was a frantic discussion about whether to ditch the advert in the light of Michael's arrest, but we decided it was probably even more important now.

With our chief fundraiser facing a criminal investigation we were in deeper trouble than ever. Only a fool would consider donating or lending money to the party in this climate, and we could no longer pretend the £4½ million was going to come in.

On the afternoon of Michael's arrest I phoned the banks. 'Houston, we have a problem,' I said cheesily, sounding like Ricky Gervais in *The Office.* 'We are just going to have to accept that we are not going to get this £4½ million in any time soon. Does that mean it will never come in? I don't know. But as of today, I can't say I am confident.'

I proposed a formal meeting the following week to discuss next steps, and suggested the banks send in someone of their choosing to oversee budget cuts. This was a desperate tightrope act. I knew the banks could just call in the receivers. I was trying to beat them to it. I knew that if I did not recommend this course of action, they would send in a team off their own bat and I would lose control. It was more than just a power game: I had one eye on how it would look to the press. If anyone discovered the banks had called in administrators it would have been a terrible story. However, 'Labour drafts in expert advice' was not quite such a bad headline.

Naively, I was still hoping that we could somehow avoid compulsory redundancies. I was hugely conscious that staff had gone to the ends of the earth to deliver savings, and the last thing I wanted was repay them by laying them off. I spent about two days kidding myself there was some other way.

At the time we had an accountant from KPMG called Jason Searancke working at HQ. The firm had a programme of seconding a member of staff to each of the political parties for experience, and he had joined us earlier that year. He was the best internal accountant the party had ever had and became a very important figure. He was completely unflappable and recognised that decision makers like myself had to be taken on a bit of a psychological journey before accepting that we were going to have to let people go. He counselled me about numbers and it was clear from our discussions that the only way that we could make the sort of savings that were necessary was by absolutely decimating the team.

The day after Michael's arrest, I asked Jason to put together a schedule showing exactly how many staff we needed to lose, over what time period, and at what cost. It was about 10.30 a.m., and I crouched down at his desk to whisper the request. There was little privacy in our open plan office and I was anxious to prevent rumours spreading.

'Get me the info by 2 p.m.,' I requested – but he sent it to me within the hour. I expect he'd prepared it earlier, and just pulled it out of a drawer.

We went into a side room and I surveyed the spreadsheet. Though I had been prepared for the numbers to be big, I was shocked to see the bottom line: we needed to axe 200 staff out of our total workforce of 340. It was likely we would also have to close one of our regional head offices. I went back to my desk clutching Jason's schedule, shell shocked.

'We've got to make 200 redundancies!' I whispered to Marianna.

'Don't be ridiculous!' she said.

'No, I am totally serious,' I hissed. I showed her Jason's piece of paper. She was horrified.

'Can you organise a senior management meeting for 3 p.m.?' I asked her. We had to start making redundancies in two weeks. She nodded. I needed to clear my head.

'I'm going out for some air,' I said. I headed onto Victoria Street. On impulse, I wandered into Westminster Cathedral, just off the grimy strip of office blocks, sandwich joints and cheap clothes shops that line the main road. I took a pew at the back of the church and sat absolutely still for about twenty minutes. I breathed in the familiar musky smell and tried to calm myself. I was devastated for the people whose lives we were about to turn upside down. I was also frightened, not knowing what the future held. I reflected on my £100,000 salary. I had really grafted to get where I was, but it was a lot of money when the party was broke. Should I make a gesture and take a pay cut? Vilma and I could clearly manage on less if we had to, but it wasn't a comfortable thought. Then there was the prospect of sacking friends. 'If I'm going to do this, I'm going to have to do it properly, and there can't be any bloody nepotism,' I thought sadly.

I wondered how No. 10 would react. I had visions of headlines about meltdown, Tony killing off the party. Our financial problems had never seemed real to many people in Downing Street. They had been hearing how broke we were for so long that it no longer meant anything. 'Now they will see what I meant when I told them we were stuffed,' I thought. I felt nauseous.

In those quiet moments at the back of the cathedral, I steeled myself for what was ahead. I drifted out and headed back down to the office feeling totally emotionally detached. 'I'm going to get on and do this,' I thought grimly. 'I've got no choice. It's my job.'

I went into a quiet room and rang Ruth. 'I know this is not what you want to hear right now, but I am going to have to make massive redundancies,' I told her.

'You can't. It will be terrible for Tony. You've got to talk to him first,' she said, sounding really shaken up.

'It's out of my hands. I've got to do it,' I replied, but we agreed to meet later that afternoon anyway and talk it over. She said she'd go and speak to Tony straight away but I made it clear I was pressing ahead with the 3 p.m. meeting with managers.

Though I'd been dreading it, the meeting was not as bad as I'd feared. I sensed that nobody was very surprised by the news. I'd always told them that if the £4½ million didn't come in we would have a problem. The reaction was quite reassuring and I felt I had a team that could deliver the changes that needed to be made.

'Over the next five days, I'd like you to quietly prepare a schedule of how many staff you think you can lose, and what function you will have left without them. Consult Jason. Tell me what cuts you can make in your departments. This is not the time to protect your own special space. And please, keep it quiet,' I told them.

About an hour later, I started receiving emails from managers, saying they were confident they could make cuts. I thought what an amazing bunch of people they were. The impossible had been asked of them time and again and they had been kicked about for months. Yet they were still responding with positive messages.

As I headed off to Downing Street to see Ruth, I felt a little better. However, Ruth was still very worried, saying redundancies on this scale would be a disaster for Tony. She reported that she'd spoken to him, and he had said I shouldn't do it.

'It's easy for him to say that, and I'm sure he genuinely means it, but there is literally nowhere else for us to go,' I replied. 'If we don't do this ourselves, it will be done to us. The banks will just go ahead and put us into administration, or worse. At least this way, we're in control.' Ruth nodded unhappily.

A few days later Tony asked to see me in his office. We sat on some wicker chairs on the veranda outside the Cabinet Office where it was totally private.

'Do we have to do this?' he asked.

'Yes, we do. We have absolutely no choice. And we might have to close Gosforth,' I said firmly. Tony appealed to me to do everything possible to avoid closing Gosforth, our Newcastle headquarters, and I agreed. He also asked me to minimise the number of job losses across the board. These were things he had to say and I respected him for going through the motions, but I had little room for manoeuvre.

I called a meeting of the NEC officers to update them on what was going on, though I didn't have much faith in their help. In fact, I felt they were partially to blame for the hole we were in. Collectively, they were supposed to be responsible for managing the party, yet they had overseen years of overspend, the consequences of which were now clear. They had been told there was a crisis over and again, but as far as they were concerned, nothing ever seemed to change: the NEC still met, they got their sandwiches at meetings, and they were still given swanky accommodation at party conferences. At their annual awayday in November, they were wined and dined. No wonder it didn't seem real. In any case, these people did not have a financial background or any particular interest in that world. Their interest was politics, and as far as they were concerned, their job was about things like selecting candidates. I felt they had failed to take any responsibility and wanted them to hear first hand how bad our situation was.

'This is real, guys. We are really going to have to lose 200 people. We are going to need permission from the banks to pay the staff in August, and they are not going to give us permission to pay 340 people,' I told them.

I had consulted an employment lawyer who had advised that we would not have to make more than the minimum statutory redundancy payments if we were at risk of bankruptcy. I told the NEC officers that we could not afford to give pay-offs, though I wanted to help people as much as I could. Most of the NEC had trade union backgrounds and had devoted careers to campaigning against employers treating staff like this, so this was particularly painful for them to hear.

I asked the NEC officers to attend the big meeting with the banks. I was planning to present an overhauled budget for the remainder of the year, and for the year ahead, 2007. The banks arranged for some big hitters from KPMG to attend. Alarmingly, they were from the company's bankruptcy team, and I had to keep reminding myself that I was the one who had suggested bringing them along. A lot was riding on it, and I didn't want to leave anything to chance, so I arranged to meet the most senior guy we dealt with at the Co-operative Bank privately a few days before the official event. I wanted to make sure he was on side and would not throw anything unexpected at us.

The man's diary was packed, and the only place he could meet us was at a crappy motel by a service station where he was staying en route to an appointment in the East Midlands. Jason, Roy and I trekked up there with overnight bags and met him in the restaurant. He did not beat about the bush.

'Look, I'm coming under huge pressure at my end to demonstrate that we're not going to lose all our money. Under normal circumstances, with other clients, we would not even be having this conversation. We'd just pull the plug,' he said.

Over the usual motorway café rubbish – steak and chips for them, a cardboardy baked potato with cheese and baked beans for me – I talked him through the scale of the job cuts we were proposing, and did my best to reassure him. It felt very bizarre to be holding a financial summit over the fate of 200 Labour Party staff in a motel.

Naively I thought the man from the bank would pay for the meal. I even made some lame joke about the restaurant probably not accepting the party's company credit card, since it was maxed out. But after coffee and a few niceties, he just upped and went, leaving me with the bill, thinking, 'That's another £60 we'll have to find.' Roy and I stayed up till about 1.30 a.m. drinking. There wasn't exactly much else to do and we ended up having quite a laugh. By the time we'd finally called it a night we had convinced ourselves that all was well with the world.

It seemed the trek to the motel was worth it, because the meeting with the banks went as I'd hoped. I gave a spiel, then the representatives from the banks backed me up, telling the NEC officers bluntly that we had no choice about the redundancies, and that if they didn't agree to the cuts we would go bankrupt. I think the bank staff were taken aback by how out of their depth the NEC officers appeared. They were joking after the NEC officers left the room about how I could work with 'that lot'.

I don't want to sound too down on the NEC, some of whom did understand the seriousness of our plight. Mike Griffiths was very supportive of me and Roy, recognising the pressure we were under. When things were really tough, he generously offered Vilma and me use of his holiday home for a break. Jeremy Beecham was also very level headed and fully understood the implications of our situation. He was very good at explaining things to other people and he was well respected by other NEC members. JP recognised the importance of the NEC taking responsibility for the problem and was hugely supportive of the staff and me in particular.

However, it is fair to say that few of them understood the mechanics of our financial situation, and KPMG were worried I might not get the support I needed to steer us through. They had concluded I was essential to delivering the recovery plan, and were afraid the NEC might turn against me, though I was confident this would not happen.

Sometime during this period I asked one of the party's lawyers to look at what would happen if we did end up going bankrupt. They discovered that, technically, members of the NEC would become personally liable for our entire debt, which was something to the tune of £35 million. They would be looking at over £1 million each. This was pretty shocking news and the implications were mind-boggling. Perhaps I should have told them – it might have concentrated their minds! There were many other questions. What assets might the banks seize? Would local party property be taken? We just didn't know. This was uncharted territory.

Solicitors acting for the creditors could have made a good case to seize anything that belonged to the party centrally or locally. It would have been a lawyers' dream. There were even discussions over whether, if we went bankrupt on one day of the week, we could reopen under a slightly different name the following day.

We tried, and failed, to compile some sort of database of all the party's property. There were buildings belonging to branches of the party all over the country, but some were derelict or unoccupied and it would have been a huge task to put together a list at a time when we had no spare resources for non-essential research.

Before pressing ahead with the job cuts, I had to seek the official approval of the entire NEC, so an emergency meeting of all thirty-two of them was called. There was little drama: they knew we had no choice, and they nodded it through. An edict went out from the chair that nobody should brief the press, and to give everyone their due, I think they realised this was not the time for mischief making. I made some token gestures at the meeting, like cancelling the sandwiches and telling everyone that the paperwork would be circulated by email because it was cheaper than printing it off.

I now had to tell the staff. I called all the Victoria Street employees into the media centre, arranging to speak to the Gosforth office staff immediately afterwards by video conference. There must have been about 120 staff in the room and all of us were nervous. I didn't see any point in beating about the bush, so I told them straight what was going on. I apologised that despite their best efforts, we would have to make very quick reductions in staff.

To my amazement, at the end of my spiel I got a round of applause. Someone put their hand up and thanked me for being so honest. I felt a lump in my throat, reflecting once again on what a great bunch of people I worked with. Here they were being told they were probably about to be laid off and yet they were thanking me. It was genuinely humbling.

Everyone drifted back to their desks and I hurried up to the boardroom to talk to the Gosforth lot. I could have jumped on a train and held the meeting in person, but I knew that by the time I arrived the news would have leaked, and I did not want staff getting the information second hand.

When I switched on the video conferencing equipment, I saw all these faces in Gosforth looking really unhappy. They knew they were more vulnerable than the people at HQ, and I had to tell them that closing their entire office was one of the options being considered. The reaction was very different to the reception I'd just had at HQ. Their prospects looked bleak, and they were not about to thank me for it. I could not give them any promises about what the future held. It was awful but I could not back away from it. Finally we issued an anodyne press release saying we were planning some restructuring, as all parties had to live within their means. Happily, nobody seemed that interested. Then we held our breath.

The big fear was that if there was a public collapse of confidence in the party's financial viability one of our lenders would freak out and demand repayment. If that happened, we were screwed. I put huge resources into trying to avoid it, ensuring we were in constant contact with each lender, listening to them as much as talking, allowing them to vent their anger and frustration about the way their generosity had backfired. I was also liaising with trade union officials who were trying to squeeze the best deal out of us for the staff. They asked if they could see our books and I was more than happy to oblige.

It's hard to describe what a difficult time this was. As the reality of the situation sank in, the atmosphere in the office became quite tense. I cancelled a holiday we'd been due to take in August. Vilma was bitterly disappointed, but there was no way I could just disappear at such a sensitive time.

I was working very closely with the team from KPMG and grew to like and respect them enormously. They threw themselves into the task, identifying savings, and seemed to enjoy the challenge. I congratulated myself on bringing them in. By the end of August, we'd shed eighty staff. The trade unions were great, recognising how desperate the situation was. They agreed to bring forward money they were due to give us later that year, which helped us limp along.

Sadly the same couldn't be said of the NEC, who still didn't seem to get it. I worried that if the banks saw how flaky they were, they would become even more jittery, and I resolved to ensure there was as little contact between them as possible. In late September, there was a discussion at Head Office over whether the banks and KPMG should sit in on a full meeting of the NEC. I concluded it would be too risky. If they were underwhelmed by the NEC officers, I feared they would be even less impressed by the rest of them. It was the right call, because at the meeting the only decision the NEC took, aside from agreeing to cancel our spring conference, was refusing to raise the fee for all conference passes. It was one of the few options open to us for increasing revenue, and for the first time, I nearly lost my temper. 'While I respect your decision, I think it's completely ridiculous,' I stormed. 'The only decision you have taken here today is to effectively decrease our income.'

My blood was boiling. Mike put his arm on my back and gave me a squeeze, a signal to calm down. I'm glad he did but I was still seething. 'If I just walked out of this job right now, wouldn't my life be a whole load easier?' I thought to myself furiously. 'Everything's going down the pan. I hardly ever see the kids, my marriage is on the rocks, and I have to work with a bunch of morons who have just voted to make things even harder for us. What the fuck is the point?'

But somehow I marched on. To the media, we put a positive spin on cancelling the spring conference, issuing a press release with some bollocks about wanting a new approach which would 'better engage the public'. Instead of one big event, we would hold a series of smaller meetings around the country, reaching out to voters over a longer period of time. We made out that the Tories were stuck in a time warp with their old-fashioned conferences. The media couldn't be bothered to challenge it.

Despite all the misery I knew I was doing my job well. The ship was almost sinking, but I was ensuring we weren't going under. My reputation in the party was soaring as I was seen to handle the crisis well. KPMG were satisfied with how we were adapting and in the autumn they issued a reassuring report to the banks. I began to think we were turning the corner.

## INTO THE ABYSS

No politician likes to admit they're heading for defeat, even when it's painfully obvious. But behind the scenes Labour has been preparing for years, just in case, to lose the next election.

Though we had escaped bankruptcy, never again could we spend money we did not have with such casual indifference. Now we were enslaved to the banks, and they wanted to know what defeat would do to our balance sheet.

As long ago as late 2006, when we were only a whisker behind the Tories in the polls, at party HQ we were drawing up budgets that assumed we might not win a fourth term. The banks needed reassurance that we would somehow keep things ticking over, however many seats were lost. Their fear was that if we just shut up shop, they would lose all the money they were owed.

We drew up a secret plan to decimate headquarters in the aftermath of a Tory victory. The document, probably still in a drawer at party HQ, detailed how we would slash back our operations leaving just a handful of staff to keep the Labour fire alight.

The banks were our masters now in a way they had never been before, and we were forced to adopt a whole new way of working. Finally, we were learning to run the party like a business. Under their guidance, we drew up a list of everything that was absolutely essential to keep the party going – key staff, buildings, heating, lighting, electricity and so on – and worked out how much it all cost. Then we drew up a second list of the income we could rely on: membership and trade union affiliation fees. Unless the money we could rely on more than covered our essential costs, we could not spend a single penny on anything else. To this day, it remains the case.

It's so obvious you would think that's how we'd have done things all along, but for years we just spent and spent as if we had a credit card with no limit. Now the banks had the power of veto over everything we did, and extras like election campaigning were a luxury that we had to negotiate.

Our very own credit crunch did not affect everyone in the party equally, however. Before becoming Prime Minister, Gordon went to some lengths to insulate himself and the Treasury from our financial troubles, setting up his own personal pot of cash at party HQ. This was money we could not dip into, since it was set aside for the Chancellor's own projects. Murray Elder helped secure donations from the Chancellor's supporters. The money was registered as a donation to the party in the normal way, but instead of going into the overall pot for general use, it went into a separate hypothecated accounting unit, which we called 'the fund with no name'. When I took over as finance director of the party in 2005, I was given an exercise book with a record of his deposits and withdrawals. All we at HQ knew was that it was for Gordon's private polling. No one asked for more detail, so I don't know if that polling was to inform Budget decisions or his long-term campaign to become party leader. Technically, there was nothing improper about it, but it always seemed strange that he should have his own stash of cash. Whenever the balance was running low, Murray would go off and secure more donations to top it up.

It was difficult for the Cabinet to come to terms with our straitened circumstances, particularly at party conferences, when they all wanted to show off. They would get totally overexcited and demand fancy videos of our achievements, or a more lavish set, none of which we could afford.

The endless competition between No. 10 and No. 11 exacerbated the problem: if No. 11 heard No. 10 was demanding some extra or other, they would want it too, and vice versa. But subtle shades of lighting and big screens all cost thousands more and they had to learn to cut their coat according to their cloth.

Whereas conference used to be a jolly affair for Labour staff, in autumn 2006 we had so few people on the payroll that we had to drag in friends and relatives to keep the show on the road. Increasingly we relied on volunteers, though for legal reasons there was no escaping paying the stewards the minimum wage. Far from being fun, it was an absolute slog, with what few staff we had left after the massive redundancy programme working crazy hours to cover up our embarrassing lack of resources. The party's conference chief, Carol Linforth, performed miracles that year, coming up with clever ways to put on a decent show on an absolute shoestring. She was so creative that few people noticed what a bargain basement event it was.

Jack gave his annual speech as treasurer of the party. As was traditional, we had written it for him at HQ, including a lot of material about what a difficult year it had been and highlighting the measures we were taking to cut costs. But Jack inserted all sorts of extra stuff about lack of governance at the heart of the party, a clear dig at No. 10. He also made some comments about our overreliance on 'rich white men' for financial support.

This felt like the last straw. In an ideal world, of course, we should be widening our donor base, and it would be great if we received a load of cash from female ethnic minorities. However, this really wasn't the time to say anything that could be interpreted as a slight to our existing donors.

I was fuming, but I wasn't entirely surprised – Jack had made a similar speech at the National Policy Forum in the ExCeL centre earlier in the year. At the time, there was someone in the auditorium I was trying to persuade to give us £1 million. I had invited him along to the NPF for a chat, but before we had a chance to talk, he'd heard Jack's comments. He was very angry and walked out of the room in the middle of the speech. I followed him and had to calm him down. He didn't give us the money. No doubt there were other reasons for his decision, but I felt sure Jack's comments had not helped.

I never raised this issue with Jack. I couldn't see the point, as his views seemed entrenched, and I didn't trust myself to keep my cool. I was already having to show an incredible amount of self-control and I knew my limits.

Our ability to spend money on anything more than wages and lightbulbs hinged on whether the small number of super-rich people we had not yet pissed off could be persuaded to take pity on us. This was highly unlikely without Michael's help. Though he had been forced to take a back seat because of his arrest, I still talked to him regularly, and he was kind enough to listen and help if he possibly could. He would ask me how it was going, and I would always reply truthfully that things were really difficult.

One day late in 2006, during another of my regular gloomy telephone conversations with him, he mentioned that Lakshmi Mittal had privately made an open offer to donate another £2 million to the party (he had given us £2 million in 2005). I was very excited to hear this, and begged him to talk to Lakshmi to firm up the pledge.

Michael was reluctant. 'How can you ask me to do that when I am having such a bloody awful time?' he asked. He was really pissed off at the way he'd been treated over 'cash for honours', and didn't feel he owed the party anything further.

'Please, Michael,' I wheedled. 'I know it's a shit time. I know you don't owe us anything. But we are really, really desperate.'

I was near enough begging and finally he gave in, agreeing to call Lakshmi and see if we could work something out. Knowing how persuasive he was, and how generous Lakshmi was towards the party, I felt sufficiently optimistic to ring the banks and tell them we might soon have £2 million coming in.

Over the weeks that followed, I kept hearing that the money was 'on its way', but it did not materialise. Michael's mood fluctuated, and it was very awkward for me having to bug him about the donation. The problem was that I didn't know Lakshmi myself, and could not really talk to him personally.

In November, after a number of further difficult exchanges between us, Michael arranged for me to talk to Lakshmi's assistant. I called her the minute I could, and she was very pleasant, but it was clear she didn't think her boss should be giving us the money. To be honest I didn't blame her. In her position, I would have been giving him exactly the same advice. Why expose yourself to all the bad publicity that donating to the Labour Party now entailed? Yet I had to push her as hard as I could.

'I hear what you're saying about it being a bad time for him to help us out, but it's got to be his call,' I said. 'Perhaps I could talk to him about it personally?' She agreed to set this up, phoning me back a little later to say that Lakshmi would call me that Saturday at 5 p.m.

I was very nervous about the call – after all, £2 million was riding on it – and I was not leaving anything to chance. I had visions of screwing up the conversation because the kids were distracting me, so I had Vilma on standby to clear the room the minute my phone rang. She was going to corral the kids into the lounge and shut the door, giving them strict orders not to emerge until I stopped talking. Everyone was poised, but 5 p.m. came and went, then 6 p.m., with no call.

By 7.30 p.m., we were all fed up waiting and I concluded he was not going to ring that night. When Vilma asked if I could nip out and get a couple of pints of milk from the corner shop, I agreed, glad to get out of the house. I left my mobile on a side table. Predictably, Lakshmi rang in the ten minutes while I was out.

'For fuck's sake!' I yelled, when Vilma told me. I didn't have his mobile number and was sure it would come up as 'withheld' on my phone.

'Calm down. He left you a number to call him back,' Vilma said.

All the kids were piled back into the sitting room as I dialled. In the event it went well. Lakshmi was very friendly, confirming that he would definitely give us the money. He said he just needed to sort out the timing. I asked him if he could put something in writing that could be shown to the banks and he agreed. A few weeks later, in early December, his letter came through.

We desperately needed the money to come in before the end of the year, but by mid-month, there was still no sign of it and radio silence from Lakshmi and his people. Feeling awful, I rang Michael for the umpteenth time, asking him whether there was any way he could chase it up again. For the first time, he got really angry. I think it must have been a particularly bad time in terms of his relationship with No. 10, and he lost it. 'What more do you want from me?' he shouted. 'I have done everything I bloody can. I'm sick of this.'

He was cross with Tony, and started complaining about how much money he'd brought into the party over the years, and how badly he'd been treated in return. I completely understood how he felt and apologised profusely for bothering him again. I could imagine the stress he was under and I resolved not to ring him about it any more.

But now I had lost my only link to Lakshmi. Though I had his mobile number, I did not feel I could use it. Feeling sick of the whole saga, I went over to No. 10 to talk to Ruth.

'Look, let's speak to Jonathan [Powell] and Tony. Maybe they can help. Jonathan knows Mr Mittal, so maybe he can talk to him. I'll have a word,' she said helpfully.

It was now almost Christmas, and Tony was about to fly to the Middle East on a five-day tour relating to the peace process. I was desperate to get the money before everyone disappeared on holiday, so I pushed for Tony or Jonathan to speak to Lakshmi while they were overseas. A few days later, I got a phone call from Jonathan saying they were at some airport and had just tried, and failed, to get hold of Lakshmi. He promised to have another go later.

That Saturday, Vilma, myself and the kids all piled off to the local garden centre to do some Christmas shopping. I was standing in the middle of the flower seeds and plant pots when Jonathan rang again to tell me Tony was on the phone to Lakshmi. He gave me a running commentary on the conversation. Suddenly, Tony grabbed Jonathan's phone.

'Hi Peter,' he said cheerfully. 'I've just spoken to Lakshmi and he was really positive. I don't see any problems. It's just a matter of time.'

I felt a bit better that Tony was involved, but I had heard this so many times before. All the same, it gave me an excuse to keep texting Lakshmi's assistant for updates.

I sent a bunch of messages but there was never any news. My texts grew more and more sheepish. 'Sorry to be a pain, but any news?' I would text; or 'You must think I'm turning into a stalker, really sorry to ask again, but is there any update?' I felt like blushing every time I pressed 'send'.

Despite all these efforts, by January 2007 there was still no sign of the £2 million, and I was going off to the USA. The State Department had invited me on an all-expenses-paid two-week trip, as part of their relationship-building programme with foreign governments, and I was really excited. The idea was to show us the US, and we whizzed around the country, from Washington to Texas, Nebraska and New York. We went to the Pentagon, and I have a cheesy video of myself standing at the rostrum. It was fantastic, but I was still fretting about the £2 million, texting and phoning Marianna every day to ask if there was any news. In Austin, Texas, I held a conference call with Jonathan and Michael on my BlackBerry, standing outside the capitol building. For some reason, Michael was back on side again, and the pair of them agreed to have one last go at persuading Lakshmi to make his donation soon.

Whatever they said, it worked, and a few days later, to universal relief, the money finally arrived.

It had taken from August until January to get this donation, and the amount of begging, cajoling and abasing myself that had been required showed what a pathetic state we had been reduced to. We were literally fighting for survival, and there was no room for pride.

Lakshmi's £2 million was immediately swallowed up as part of the 2006 budget, and the whole fundraising cycle began again for the year ahead. As a result of our heavy cost cutting, we had far less to raise than in previous years, and Jane Hogarth and I had lined up £1½ million in small donations. We had spent many hours hitting the phones to potential supporters, arranging for a small group of donors to help by finding other wealthy individuals to match gifts they had agreed to make themselves, ranging between £25,000 and £250,000. This was quite a cunning way of raising money, as it meant these supporters were doing the graft, persuading other rich folk to part with their cash. I suppose the people they approached probably felt some peer pressure to show they were rich enough to compete. The system was very successful, bringing in most of the money we needed for 2007.

Another way we raised funds that year was through private dinners organised by me and Ruth. We had never had to do it before, as the events had always been Michael's gig. It was bloody hard work, but great fun, and very effective. Tony came along, as did Hazel Blears, now party chair, and both of them were brilliant at helping charm the donors. At a time when everyone else was running away from fundraising for Labour because it was so politically toxic, Hazel and Tony never gave up, and through these dinners, we raised substantial sums.

I was hugely grateful for Hazel's support during this period. Her job chairing the party during these dark days was endlessly challenging but she always put on a brave and cheerful face and made time for other people.

I remember meeting her in an upstairs room in Downing Street a few minutes after Tony had told her she was being promoted to the Cabinet, as party chair, in May 2006, and we had a funny exchange about what she'd let herself in for. I congratulated her and told her it was a bloody tough job.

'Can't be worse than the other jobs I've had,' she joked. A couple of months later I reminded her of that comment, and she agreed I'd been right.

She always went out of her way to tell people what a great job I was doing, and seemed to be one of the few people who really understood the toxic implications of the 'cash for honours' affair and our huge debts. In my darkest hours, I was able to use her as a sounding board, and at times she kept me sane. While most people seemed to be burying their heads in the sand, Hazel threw her weight behind everything I was doing, backing me up over the job losses and budget cuts. Despite being a Cabinet minister she was ready to make sacrifices herself, never taking taxis unless she was paying the fare out of her own pocket, never claiming any expenses, and keeping the absolute minimum of staff. It's ironic that she was later castigated over her parliamentary expenses – the Hazel I knew was frugal, and the accusations against her never sounded right.

As a result of all this effort, by spring 2007 we only needed to find another £500,000 for the rest of the year, an achievable sum. I was feeling pretty good. Yes, money was tight, but we had adapted to our diminished means, in some cases actually delivering more for less money. The crisis had forced us to sort out our priorities, and the party had become a slicker machine.

I was beginning to feel very powerful. I credited myself with saving the party from bankruptcy and revelled in how I'd coped. 'It doesn't matter what shit is thrown at me, I can survive,' I thought, as my head swelled. I was beginning to live in a fantasy world in which I was indispensable to the party. In my own mind, I was untouchable. This was a very dangerous place to be, and I was sowing the seeds of my own destruction.

Though the party was finally back on something resembling stable foundations financially, I knew the whole edifice was built on sand. Any unexpected demands such as a sudden by-election or leadership contest could spell disaster – and sure enough, they did. It happened when some of the lenders began demanding their money back.

Sir Christopher Evans, who had been arrested and released without charge over 'cash for honours', was furious at his treatment and wanted the £1 million he'd lent to be repaid right away. Under the circumstances we could hardly argue, so we scraped together the money to settle the debt. We had always feared that once one lender broke ranks others would follow suit, and that was exactly what happened. As the dreaded annual audit approached in May, two more individuals started asking for their money back too: another £2 million we had to find. Once again, we faced bankruptcy and I was forced to go through the whole desperate process of securing guarantees from lenders to get our accounts signed off.

That summer, as Gordon took over, we began negotiating a long-term settlement with the lenders to spare us this horrendous annual ritual. By autumn, we had persuaded most of the lenders to defer payment for a significant period of time. But one individual still wanted his money back fast.

One Tuesday, I received a hand-delivered letter from his lawyers warning that unless we agreed a satisfactory repayment schedule, he would have to consider what course of action to take. This was clearly a threat to take us to court.

'Fuck,' I exclaimed, as I read the letter. I showed it to Marianna. 'We're about to be sued for £1 million.'

'Shit,' she replied.

'We're fucked,' I said.

If he pressed ahead with his threat, we both knew the whole pack of cards would come crashing down. The minute they got wind of it, other lenders would almost certainly panic and pile in with their own demands. If that happened, there was no way we could carry on as normal. We would have been knowingly trading when insolvent – a criminal offence.

Heart pounding, I got straight on the phone to one of the party's solicitors, and then informed KPMG. An urgent meeting was arranged for the following Tuesday to thrash out a strategy. But I was spared the pleasure of attending, for on the Monday, I resigned.

# 8. COLLEAGUES OR COMRADES?

We were badly damaged and desperate to regain the initiative as the 'cash for honours' scandal raged, so Tony did what politicians in a hole usually do, and announced an independent inquiry by an establishment grandee.

However, the cross-party review of party funding led by Sir Hayden Phillips, which could have paved the way for historic change, was doomed from the start – not least because the Prime Minister failed to tell anyone in the Labour Party machine he was going to do it before dashing off the press release.

'What the hell is this all about?' exclaimed Mike Griffiths at the next NEC meeting. 'He could at least have told us!'

Others waded in, angrily accusing the Prime Minister of opening an inquiry that would inevitably raise questions about the relationship between the Labour Party and the trade unions when as far as they were concerned the real problem was our dealings with millionaires.

'This party has had more than 100 years of transparent funding from the trade unions. There's no need to attack them. If you just stop the millionaire donors, there won't be a problem,' Jack Dromey said angrily, to nods of agreement.

He was right: the heavy dependence on the generosity of these billionaires and millionaires was dangerous for all three parties, regularly leading to allegations of corruption or the buying of influence. Sir Hayden's review was designed to address this.

The problem was that the system could not be overhauled without some loosening of the ties between Labour and the trade unions, which together contributed around £11 million a year to our coffers. Unfortunately, that was unthinkable to large swathes of the party. By this stage in his premiership Tony was too weak to force the issue, and it was not in Gordon's interests to help. Had he wanted, the Chancellor could probably have strong-armed the party into making concessions that would have saved Sir Hayden's review. However, Gordon Brown had nothing to gain from picking this fight. He needed the support of the trade unions to become Prime Minister, his primary focus, and they would not throw their weight behind him if he was seen to be encouraging attempts to reduce their influence. Now was not the time for him to rock the boat. As a result, the review, launched in March 2006 with genuinely good intentions, quickly descended into acrimony and farce.

Along with Jack Straw, I represented the Labour Party at the various private meetings. There were confidential discussions with Sir Hayden, meetings of a cross-party committee and bilateral meetings between the main parties.

Sometimes the discussions bordered on the absurd, such as when we managed to clinch a deal with the Lib Dems by promising that Menzies (Ming) Campbell would get a taxpayer-funded car and driver if the reforms went through. On other occasions, there were ugly scenes with the Tories, such as the time an exasperated Francis Maude turned on us in one of the final sessions of the cross-party meetings.

'Unless the Labour Party understands that you can't ban rich individuals from giving large sums to parties when the trade unions do the same, then it is difficult to see how we will make any progress,' he shouted.

'Don't patronise us!' I spat back. 'We've been trying to understand each other's position for months, and now right at the end, you are throwing it all back at us.'

I knew the Conservatives were preparing to blame us for the collapse of the talks, and though they were probably right, I felt Maude had failed to grasp the immensity of the challenge Jack and I faced to persuade our own party to accept change.

Still, my primary emotion during the process was intense frustration, because my own party was the biggest block to reform.

To the public, reading media reports of our apparent refusal to budge over the unions, we must have seemed quite unreasonable, especially as the Conservatives seemed ready to make radical reforms. Most eye-catching was their proposal to introduce a £50,000 cap on donations from individual donors, a move that would have had a huge impact on their own revenue, turning off the taps from their billionaire benefactor Lord Ashcroft. Labour's failure to give ground on anything like this scale must have looked pathetic by comparison.

However, what the public struggled to understand was that Labour was not just 'linked' to the trade unions: we were inextricably bound up with them, like one of those rubber band balls. If you tried to unpick the ball, to remove the 'trade union' threads, the ball would completely disintegrate. The unions, which along with the Fabians formed the Labour Party in the early twentieth century, had twelve seats on the 32-strong NEC, and controlled 50 per cent of the vote on policy issues. They were part of the DNA of the party, and we could not simply cut them out. It would literally risk breaking up the party.

Moreover, the seven-figure donations we received from these organisations ultimately came from hundreds of thousands of individual workers, each of whom paid a pound or two into their union's 'political fund'. The way most people in the Labour Party saw it, when a union like Amicus gave us £1 million, it was actually 700,000 different people each giving the party less than £1.50. Viewed that way, it was not hard to see why the suggestion that this funding stream should be blocked was so bitterly resisted.

The great hope was that a different and more transparent system could be devised for those workers to continue giving their financial support, so that it was possible to trace each little donation to an individual, but that was not as easy as it sounded.

The talks began with a cordial meeting between Tony and Ming in No. 10, in which the Lib Dem leader agreed that it was right to attempt to change the system. As the smallest of the three main parties they had the most to gain from fundamental reforms, particularly a significant extension of state funding, something Tony was keen on.

A preliminary meeting between the PM and David Cameron was more delicate. They met on neutral territory in the House of Commons, Tony sweeping into the room with a large retinue of staff, myself included. Cameron, who had been leader of his party for less than a year, was accompanied by just two aides and looked very much the junior figure. It must have been hard for him not to be intimidated. Tony mischievously made a great performance of being very laid back and dismissive, his body language suggesting he was doing everyone a great favour by merely attending. We all knew it was just showmanship, but it must have made the encounter more daunting for the young Tory leader.

During their brief discussion, the PM and Cameron agreed to enter into the review with open minds, both saying they were prepared to consider any measures to bring an end to the scandals associated with taking large sums money from tycoons.

'Of course, you're going to have to allow some discussions about trade union funding,' Cameron told Tony boldly.

'Of course, you'll have to look at millionaire and company funding,' Tony retorted, a clear reference to Ashcroft and his businesses. He added that he was fully committed to the review, but couldn't resist emphasising that he was rather busier than the opposition leader, so might not have as much time to be personally involved.

The No. 10 team played along with his theatrics. After about fifteen minutes, an aide made a great show of whispering in the Prime Minister's ear that he was needed elsewhere, and along with his huge entourage, he disappeared. It was all a game, and to his credit, Cameron did not seem too fazed. I was impressed by him.

Before the process went any further, the NEC called an emergency meeting to confront Tony about launching the review without consulting them. They were full of bravado in the run-up, threatening a big showdown with the Prime Minister. But as soon as he strode into the room, all brisk and genial, you could see their resolve evaporating. His great skill was in making whatever he wanted to do sound so reasonable.

'The relationship between the Labour Party and the trade unions is sacrosanct,' he said soothingly. 'What we're talking about here is our financial relationship with them. The public has lost faith in the way political parties are funded, so we have to do something.'

They were sufficiently mollified to hold their tongues while he was in the room, but as soon as he left, they erupted again. They thought it was unfair that the trade unions were going to come under attack for a problem that was not of their making. Privately, they blamed Matthew Taylor, No. 10's head of policy, as much as Tony for instigating the review. They had not forgotten a pamphlet he once wrote which called for the abolition of the trade union 'block vote' on party policy, and the end of so-called 'affiliated membership', the term given to people who join the party through a trade union. Ever since, he had been viewed as a deeply suspicious figure.

For all his soothing words to the NEC, privately the Prime Minister had long wanted to reform Labour's relationship with the trade unions and was ready to 'think the unthinkable'. He believed we needed to re-examine the way decisions were taken in the party and consider whether the trade unions should have such a major role in the process. He disliked the huge power of the trade union barons, who could practically dictate party policy.

He thought the relationship should become 'more modern' – a term the unions correctly interpreted as meaning they would be less influential. As far as he was concerned, this was a glittering opportunity to push through changes that would have been inconceivable had the party not been so shaken by 'cash for honours'.

I also disliked the extent to which we had to dance to the unions' tune. I remember an occasion when one union, Unite, left it until the last minute to book a stand at one of our party conferences. As a result, they were given a very poor spot in the corner of the exhibition hall. When the union's boss, Derek Simpson, turned up the night before conference opened and saw his sorry little stand, he went ballistic. 'I don't give my millions to the party for my stand to be stuck in a bloody corner,' he bellowed. 'You better get this sorted right now.'

I had not realised the stand was in such a poor location, and privately I agreed with him. However, all the units were now in place – scores and scores of them – and there was no way we could just shift them around to find a better spot for his display. They were very heavy structures. On the other hand we could not afford a rift with Derek, so staff literally worked through the night to build him a 'satellite' stand at the top of the stairs by the entrance. It was the first display delegates would see as they arrived. Derek was still acting all offended, so to smooth his ruffled feathers, we arranged extra adverts for Unite in all the conference literature. I can think of no other body with the power to cause so much turmoil the night before the most important event in our calendar.

Even the Prime Minister had to kowtow to these characters. I remember an event Tony hosted at Downing Street to thank the trade unions for their support in the 2005 general election. Most of the guests were not exactly fans. After the formalities were over, the Prime Minister found himself playing second fiddle to Tony Woodley, the joint general secretary of Amicus. As well as heading the biggest trade union, Woodley was chair of the affiliated trade unions' umbrella organisation, TULO, and soon he was holding court. It was probably the only time the Prime Minister found himself usurped at his own reception.

Knowing I leaned towards Tony's point of view, some people on the NEC did not trust me to represent the interests of the trade unions fairly, so they set up a separate committee to keep an eye on what Jack and I were doing. We used to have to go along to their meetings and explain ourselves, and they would caution us against giving any ground. It is hard to overstate the level of paranoia. The unions feared they were in serious danger of losing their ability to influence policy and manoeuvre their candidates into parliamentary seats, challenging what for them was the purpose of their relationship with the party.

Before we had even met Sir Hayden, the review was threatening to plunge Labour into bitter internal warfare. The question for us was who ran the party. Was it jacket and no tie, or sharp suits and cufflinks? Were we colleagues or comrades?

Gordon's view was that Tony and his friends were responsible for getting the party into this mess. The Chancellor went out of his way to avoid Michael Levy, refusing point blank when I asked whether he would meet him.

'Absolutely not,' he huffed indignantly. He believed that the perception of sleaze would disappear as soon as he took over from Tony. This was partly true – for while Tony enjoyed the company of the international jet set and had extravagant tastes, holidaying on expensive yachts and playing the property market, Gordon had successfully cultivated a hair-shirt image. Whatever else the public thought of him, they did not see him as sleazy.

None the less, the Chancellor had a tricky balancing act. He did not know whether the leadership would be contested when Tony stepped down and was trying to please everyone. While internally he needed to be seen to be supporting the unions, publicly he could not risk looking too much of an 'old lefty'. His strategy was to keep out of it.

'Now isn't the time to revisit the relationship with the trade unions,' he said dismissively, in one of the regular private meetings I had with him in the run-up to the transition. He liked to observe that Tony did not have enough support in the party to deliver internal reforms, which was true. However, he was too weak only because the Chancellor would not support him.

When I eventually met Sir Hayden, I had a clear set of instructions from the NEC, and a clear set from Tony, and they were largely incompatible. I liked Sir Hayden immediately: he was a proper career civil servant who fully recognised the magnitude of his task. He was under no illusions about the prospects of achieving a consensus, but seemed determined to give it his best shot. He hoped that he could swing things by sheer force of personality, but he recognised that dealing with the party leaders was the easy bit – none of it would come to anything if they could not bring their parties with them.

The first six weeks of the review were designed to help the parties understand each other's funding systems. Such was the level of mistrust within the Labour Party that every time we at HQ submitted written evidence to Sir Hayden, the trade unions submitted a separate paper. TULO began running a campaign to save the 'affiliated relationship', the system under which the unions paid a collective membership fee to Labour and effectively bought a stake in the party. They saw the review as 'Blairites taking over the party' and were determined to block progress.

I found it all excruciatingly embarrassing. Though few people knew it, the Labour Party was on the verge of bankruptcy at the time, and if someone had offered me state funding at that point, I would have bitten off their hand. 'Cash for honours' had killed off our revenue from rich donors, but millionaires were still pouring their cash into Tory coffers. I knew that if we did not reform the system, the Tories would continue to build up a huge war chest, while we would struggle just to pay our everyday bills. The status quo would put us at a catastrophic disadvantage come the next general election. I did not feel we could afford to lose this unique opportunity to impose a donation cap.

In the months that followed, there were numerous cross-party meetings, with Francis and Andrew Tyrie for the Tories, and Archy Kirkwood and David Heath for the Lib Dems. It was all quite jolly at first, but these formal meetings were not where the real negotiating took place: they were more about showing off. Jack played reasonable, I played hardball, but we never really got anywhere.

The amount of time and resources directed at the review was enormous. Civil servants spent weeks examining the complex internal financing structures of the trade unions and devising alternative models. There were endless debates over whether workers were fully aware that the money they paid into their union's political fund ended up in Labour Party coffers. You would have thought it would be quite simple just to get each member to pay the money to us directly, but that would have reduced the power of the general secretaries to give and withdraw funding to us at their discretion. Naturally they prized their ability to dispense largesse.

As time went by, it became painfully obvious that the Labour Party could not resolve its internal issues and cross-party consensus was impossible. Tony became increasingly exasperated with Gordon's refusal to intervene. Jack and I would meet him occasionally to update him on progress, and the Prime Minister would stress that he was prepared to take all the flak from the trade unions if Gordon would just help behind the scenes.

'I don't know why Gordon doesn't just let me get on with it, and I'll take all the shit. We have to do it, we have got to reform,' he would say despairingly.

But the momentum was slipping away.

*

While Gordon had refused to throw his weight behind the Hayden Phillips review, as the transition approached, the Chancellor became increasingly preoccupied by the power of the unions for another reason.

He feared his first party conference as leader could be overshadowed by embarrassing policy defeats as a result of the block vote and was dreading the thought of sitting though the annual 'torture-the-leader session by the sea'. Letting, or even encouraging, the unions to punish Tony was one thing, but it was not something he fancied experiencing himself. Of course he couldn't say so publicly before he became leader, and in the past, he had repeatedly warned the Prime Minister he would block any attempt to reduce the unions' power. He hoped they would be grateful for his defence. However, in the months before he took over he asked me privately if I would begin preparing the necessary rule changes and justifications for reducing the size of the block vote so that the unions could no longer defeat the government at will.

On one occasion I took him the draft plan and he became incredibly twitchy that his scheme would leak. 'Who has seen it? Who has it been emailed to?' he demanded.

I put a great deal of work into this project for him, and preparations were in place before Tony left. Gordon was secretly hoping to use the honeymoon period after he took over to push the changes through via a ballot of the whole party.

Initially, he was very bullish. The likely scenarios had all been played through – what if the NEC tried to stop him? What if a trade union went to the courts? The strategy was simple: Gordon was going to be strong and stand up to his detractors in the party and force the issue.

However, once he became leader, he quickly realised compromise was best, and over the summer of 2007 negotiations with the trade unions began. The talks dragged on for weeks without progress, and he became increasingly agitated. The issue had turned into a trial of strength.

Negotiations were led by Joe Irvine from No. 10, with support from Jonathan Ashworth in the No. 10 political office and myself. It was obvious that the new leader and his team had underestimated how tricky it was negotiating with the unions. There were fraught sessions behind closed doors when Joe and I were tongue lashed by senior trade union officials. We reported back to Gordon, who was becoming less up for the fight. He did not want to risk humiliation and was desperate to compromise, while talking tough. He would shout at us and then concede something. We would report the concession back to the trade unions and they would demand he give more ground. We would report back, he would shout at us again and then make a further concession. And so it went on.

A week before party conference began, the issue was still not resolved. Jonathan Ashworth and I finished a meeting with the trade unions in Downing Street at about 10.30 p.m. Gordon was in the Downing Street flat so we went upstairs to tell him the latest progress. We found him and Sarah having had a small dinner party. It was cheerful and chaotic, with washing up piled high in the cramped kitchen and dirty crockery everywhere. Gordon greeted me warmly and offered me a glass of champagne, which I accepted. He rummaged around in the cupboards for a clean glass but all he could find were some mugs, so I stood there drinking champagne out of a coffee cup until Sarah arrived and found something more appropriate. I found his shambolic approach rather endearing.

Over the coming days, we reached a compromise over the block vote. It would stay, but the impact of a government defeat at conference was watered down, with the rules formally recognising the right of the leadership to ignore it. The unions were pleased that they had retained their right to defeat the leadership, however meaninglessly.

On this, and on the Hayden Phillips review, the unions won. On 30 October 2007, around eighteen months after the review was launched, the cross-party talks finally collapsed after a particularly acrimonious meeting. In press statements, Jack accused the Tories of being 'unwilling to negotiate' while Francis Maude complained that his party had 'come up against an absolute brick wall'. The Lib Dems blamed the Conservatives, accusing them of 'walking away'.

Sir Hayden announced that he would publish a report anyway, setting out a number of alternative party funding models for future discussion, but we all knew it would be kicked into the long grass.

Though the unions greeted the suspension of the talks with great glee, the failure to reach any agreement was a disaster for the Labour Party. The introduction of state funding would have solved our financial crisis; there was no Plan B. We were now in for the long haul and would have to watch helplessly as the Tories amassed a fortune from their wealthy supporters to fight the next election campaign, while we continued to rely on the benevolence of the trade unions. While donations from tycoons could not come with strings attached, the trade union barons were never shy of articulating what they expected in return.

# 9. DAD

At 6.45 p.m. on 4 July 2007, my father died surrounded by his family in the downstairs front room of our family house in Poole. He was sixty-one. We were all there, children and grandchildren – probably about twenty people in total. My brother Tim said a prayer and we all left Mum to spend some time alone with the man who had shared her life for nearly forty years.

Dad became terminally ill at what was already a hugely difficult time for me. At work, I was coping with the combined pressures of 'cash for honours', the leadership transition and the party's ongoing financial crisis. At home, my marriage was in trouble.

Strangely, however, good things came of Dad's passing.

How you cope and feel about the death of a loved one can have a lot to do with how other people react. As a family we all rallied around each other, and though it was obviously a devastating period, in many ways we found the experience curiously positive and reaffirming. We remembered that we were a loving and strong family and coped together, and Vilma and I remembered why we loved each other.

Equally, colleagues rallied around. Marianna, Roy, Alicia, Anouska and Hilary all protected me and helped me prioritise family at a time when, left to my own devices, I probably would have failed to get the balance right. Perhaps more surprisingly, a number of very senior politicians chose to share in our family trauma, and put themselves out for Mum and Dad, and for me. The way they reacted to Dad's illness and death showed them at their best.

The warmth and kindness Tony, JP, Ian McCartney, Hazel and

Gordon showed my family was a source of great strength to my parents, and made me proud of what I did. Despite all the pressure and all the tension, we stood together when it really mattered. It made the sense of betrayal all the greater when Gordon threw me to the wolves a mere four months later.

The last few years hadn't been easy for either of my parents. It was all such a surprise. For years Dad had been so healthy, running marathons and enjoying hiking through the Dorset countryside and coastal paths. And then in 2004 he had been diagnosed with a rare cancer in his shoulder and had undergone two lots of major surgery that left him with no cancer but no right shoulder. He'd always been a workaholic and so the resultant enforced retirement came as a bit of a shock to both my parents. Looking back, I think Dad coped with it better than Mum. They were still active foster carers, and with my brother Toby and sister Amber still at school, there were six children in the house in total. For Dad, retirement meant new challenges – like reorganising the house, creating order and structuring Mum's day. Not unreasonably, Mum felt that she had managed perfectly well organising and structuring her time for more than thirty years without Dad's enthusiastic input.

The truth was that Dad was an enigma – on the one hand loving, caring and proud of his family, and on the other a moody, occasionally rude and stubborn sod. Mum called him Victor – as in Meldrew – and it was a pretty accurate description. Whatever else he was, though, Dad was my friend and like most friends we had our ups and downs. There were times over the years when we went through long periods of not speaking, sometimes my fault, sometimes his.

However, when I was stressed and needed someone to talk things through, it was Dad I called, and he would listen. If the stress or problem was mild to moderate then I'd pop down to Poole and we would go for a pint at the Tatnam pub. More serious discussion meant a walk along the Dorset Coast Path, where we would put the world to rights in stunning scenery followed by a pint at a pub in Swanage or Corfe. It was closeness but not an intimate closeness: for a lifelong socialist and long-time Labour Party member, Dad was very conservative. I think that if you asked any of my brothers and sisters they would feel the same: he wasn't an easy man, but we loved him and he loved us.

The funny thing was that his illness seemed to mellow him and as he slowly recovered from the surgery to his shoulder he seemed to relax. He began to plan his future and had started studying to be a deacon, a lay position in the Catholic Church. It kept him busy, and that suited Mum as well. Then in the summer of 2006 he began to feel poorly – a bit weak and sleepy and off his food. It did not seem anything too serious and, as always, he was stoical. Naturally, we all worried that the cancer might have returned, but a few tests and a kidney biopsy showed a benign problem, glomerular nephritis. We all breathed easier as he was given steroids in full expectation that he would begin to feel better.

Christmas came and went and I was immersed in work – 'cash for honours' rolled on, fundraising was a priority, the trade unions were battling to block reforms to party funding and we were planning for a leadership election. I was also planning a two-week study visit to the United States in early January.

When I returned from my visit to America, I received a call from my sister Gerry. While I had been obsessing about work and enjoying my stint in the States, there was bad news at home. The steroids had not made Dad feel better, he wasn't eating, was in pain, had had several falls and was spending increasing amounts of time in bed. Mum was at her wits' end and Gerry was very worried about how she was coping. The truth was that I hadn't even noticed that my parents were having such a bad time. While I was busy being important, Berni, Gerry, her partner Franki, my brother Damien and his wife Janice were spending more and more time supporting them.

I spoke to Vilma and we agreed that I should go down to Poole for a couple of days. When I got there I was shocked. Dad looked rough and Mum exhausted. I went and sat with him upstairs in his room and we watched some sport and talked. He was scared and admitted that he thought that he had cancer again. He was certainly depressed and had lost weight. We talked about Mum and how stressed she was and he agreed to go to the doctor again. And then Dad cried. My proud, stubborn and sometimes emotionally cold father cried. It was an appalling moment for both of us – we should have hugged but there was nearly forty years of learnt behaviour at play. We had to settle for holding hands.

Back at home Vilma and I were also having a rough time. For years we had been trying to have our own baby. We both had children from previous marriages and loved them all but we wanted a little 'Peter and Vilma'. It just didn't happen. Tests showed no obvious reason – we'd both had children before, just not together. We'd been on a waiting list for IVF and finally in early 2007 we got a date to start. Nobody else on my side of the family knew about this very private issue. It should have been an emotional burden we shared equally, but with hindsight I was more focused on work than our fertility problems and left Vilma to manage most of the process alone, even if on occasion I managed to attend appointments.

In February, Vilma underwent daily injections in preparation for egg collection. It was a strange process. The eggs were harvested under general anaesthetic and then I had to take them in a taxi, along with a sperm sample, to the clinic where fertilisation would happen. I got there and nervously handed over the incubator containing the eggs and sperm, and was told to sit down in an absolutely packed waiting room. Ten minutes later my name was called and I proudly stood up, making it clear I was Mr Watt.

The nurse said loudly, 'I'm sorry but the sperm was really poor quality. You can either pop to a cubicle and produce another specimen or we can make do.'

'Make do,' I squeaked, horrified, and ran out.

Two days later Vilma had fertilised eggs implanted and we waited with everything crossed. A fortnight later a pregnancy test was negative and, as there were no more viable embryos available from this cycle, we faced another round of injections, another egg collection and more waiting and hoping.

In early March, after a succession of visits to his GP, Dr Oxley, Dad was booked to have a scan of his left kidney. A couple of days later he went to see Dr Oxley for the results. The appointment was at 10 a.m. and he had promised to phone as soon as he could. I delayed going to work in order to take the call. At 10.45 the phone rang, and Mum said she had Dad with her.

'They've found a tumour. It's the size of a small orange,' the doctor said.

His voice was cracking with emotion. I can't really remember what either of us said next, but I know he told me he was going to ring everyone himself and break the news. When I told Vilma, she was determinedly optimistic, saying there was a chance it might not be cancer, but I was in no doubt. It was classic Vilma and me – she buried her head pretending it wasn't happening, while I became cold and practical. I'm not sure I'd recommend either strategy, to be honest.

I decided to call all the family myself and give them the benefit of my realism. Vilma and I went for a pub lunch at the Shire Horse, up the road from our home, and I hit the phone. My brother Phil later told me he thought I was a miserable bastard during this phone call, as he was still feeling positive and thought I was exaggerating. I think I was seeking comfort in being the older brother to everyone and being 'sensible'. It felt easier than crying.

Over the next few weeks Mum was inundated with calls from the family. On the one hand I'm sure it was great but on the other hand it was hard work for her. So we persuaded her to start a blog, where she could keep everyone updated on Dad's condition. In March 2007 she started the Watt Blog?, where over the next six months she recorded what happened and how she felt. It became the place where we would all go several times a day to get a fix of family, to support Mum and to support each other.

At 3.30 p.m. on 29 March, three days after the blog started, Dad went for a biopsy of his kidney. We all checked back regularly for details and after an overnight stay Dad came out of hospital and we all waited for news. I'd like to say that I was totally distracted at work worrying about my parents, but to be honest, in a classic case of warped priorities, I wasn't. I was compartmentalising my life to a degree that with hindsight was completely unhealthy.

The results of the biopsy were due on 5 April. I was at work. At about 10 a.m., I got a call from Dad. I went to a quiet room. He could hardly talk, and when he finally got his words out he said, 'It's cancer.'

I called Vilma and told her, crying as I spoke.

A week later, on 12 April, Dad saw a surgeon who said that the tumour was inoperable and that he had between six and eight months to live. Suddenly it was all very real. My dad was dying. The truth is that I was also secretly relieved that the 6–8 months prognosis meant that there was a good chance I would be able to manage the local and Scottish elections in May and, fingers crossed, the leadership election. I can hardly believe that this even entered my head, but the truth is it did. What kind of creature had I become?

The next couple of months was a blur as I tried to balance work, home and travelling down to Poole to see my parents a couple of times a week. Vilma was all too often left on her own with the kids during the week and we went for days at a time without seeing each other. Most weekends, however, we packed the car and drove down the M3 and M27 together to see Mum and Dad.

Dad began to keep an audio diary on a digital recorder and Mum was by now an active blogger, keeping everyone up to date and getting things off her chest, while we all made comments, often inappropriate. It was going to be a thoroughly modern death. The extended family of nine brothers and sisters and their partners, friends and children probably saw more of each other than they had done for years. In some ways we almost began to enjoy the whole thing.

It was particularly lovely that I was able to develop a closeness with Dad that I hadn't had for years. We would pop out to the Tatnam late on an evening and have a couple of pints. We would talk about life, Mum and my work. He was always interested in what was going on in the Labour Party. Often Gerry and Franki would come and Dad developed an appalling sense of humour. One evening in the pub we bumped into a mate of his he hadn't seen for a few months. He bought Dad a pint and asked Dad how he was as he had heard he had been under the weather. With a completely straight face Dad replied, 'Not so good, actually. I've got cancer and will be dead in a few months, but thanks for the pint.' He came and sat down chuckling at the look on his friend's face. On another occasion we went for an Indian take-away after a few pints. The staff knew him as a regular and Dad reckoned he would get a discount on the order if he told them about his illness and prognosis. He told them and they were very sympathetic but still charged him full price.

One weekend in early May the whole family – about thirty of us – was in Poole. The house was so crowded we had to hold meals in three sittings. On the Saturday evening Tim, Dad, Phil and I went off in the car to meet Damien at a pub just outside Poole. On the way over we pulled off the road to get directions and Dad, who was sitting in the front seat, decided to get out and stretch his legs. He opened the door and tried to get out but somehow he couldn't make it and, with me watching from the back seat, nearly fell out head first. I didn't understand what was happening – I think I thought he was just mucking around – but Phil, who was in the driver's seat, realised he was keeling over. Between them, he and Tim, who had got out of the car, managed to catch him and push him upright.

We all laughed at my failure to react but it was clear that Dad was struggling. He was obviously weaker, had lost even more weight and he was drowsy. His pain levels were up and he was taking more and more morphine. The following day we all went to see my son Ben play cricket and Dad was obviously in pain the entire time we were there. Ben was bowled out for a duck but took six wickets for six runs – his dad and granddad were very proud.

Back at work the pressure was still on as the financial situation remained dire and the leadership transition was fast approaching. People knew what was happening with Dad and they were supportive in helping me leave early or take work home. Hazel wrote to Mum and Dad and called them, as did Ian. I know that Mum and Dad really appreciated this. JP also called them on several occasions, having extended conversations with them both. Mum is his biggest fan to this day. Gordon wrote a really personal letter to them and sent an inscribed copy of his book *Courage*. He spent ages writing the letter, determined to get it right and I got several phone calls from his office checking facts for inclusion. It was incredibly thoughtful.

I was also very moved that despite all the pressure they were under themselves, Hazel, Ian, JP and Gordon all took the time to contact my parents. I know how proud and touched Mum and Dad were. The icing on the cake came on 15 May, when they were invited to No. 10. Franki drove them up to our house in Chessington and Vilma cooked them lunch and at about 1 p.m. a taxi drove them to Downing Street. Ruth met them, took them in and made them coffee. I walked over from Victoria Street and met them there. We were all sitting in Ruth's office with Mum and Dad on their best behaviour, not quite believing they were there. They were so engrossed talking to Ruth that they didn't notice Tony walk in – their faces when they saw him were a picture.

Tony stayed with us for half an hour and chatted. He told them what a great job I was doing and I reminded him that I was his second choice for General Secretary. Mum and Dad were appalled at my rudeness but Tony laughed. He took them into the Cabinet room and sat Dad in the PM's chair. The photo is up in Mum's front room.

One of Tony's staff, Jonathan Pearce, then gave them one of his famous Downing Street tours. Though Dad was getting very tired, he was determined to walk all the way. They left in another taxi, which took them back to Chessington. Vilma said that when they arrived, Dad was still on a real high despite his exhaustion, and told her all about it before Franki drove them home to Poole.

It was the one and only time that they got a glimpse of what my life at work was like. I know how proud they were that day, and I was proud of them.

In late May, Vilma and I began another cycle of IVF. Or rather, Vilma started another cycle of IVF, since once again I wasn't there to support her. The second half of May was a rough time for Dad too, as his condition deteriorated and his pain increased. He spent more and more time sleeping. My parents were being supported by the Macmillan Nurses team and the local hospice, Forest Home.

Time sped by at work as Tony announced his resignation date and the leadership and deputy leadership election began. I'd never been so busy, and I wasn't able to get down to see Mum and Dad as much. The result was that I missed some big family occasions, including the family house Mass on 9 June. It was held in Mum and Dad's back garden and Fr Mark from their church said the Mass. Dad in particular loved the day. During the weekend of the official handover from Tony to Gordon in late June, my parents went to see Tim and Jayne in Newcastle for their daughter Megan's first Holy Communion. Dad was becoming weaker and weaker, and it was not an easy weekend. At the house in Poole a stair lift was installed as he could no longer get upstairs without help. When I was able to get down we still managed to get to the pub but it often took quite a while to walk the short distance there. Often Dad wouldn't finish his pint – a cardinal sin in our family – and would fall asleep in the middle of a sentence.

The week before the end of the leadership and deputy leadership contest, Vilma underwent egg collection and fertilisation again. On Friday 22 June fertilised embryos were transferred, and we braced ourselves for the very difficult two-week wait to find out whether the treatment had succeeded this time and she was pregnant.

The weekend after Mum and Dad's Newcastle trip we all decided to meet at their place. The house was packed – everyone was there.

For years there had been real tension between Vilma and me on the one hand, and my former wife Donna on the other. This clearly wasn't easy for anyone in the family. Donna was still really close to my parents and my brothers and sisters, and she lived in Poole with our children Ben and Anya, near them all. It had been really difficult for Vilma and me whenever we visited my parents, as Donna would often be around. It was always uncomfortable for Ben, Anya and my step-daughter Ivanna, Vilma's daughter by her first marriage. It had regularly caused tension between Vilma and me.

Yet that weekend, as we all gathered to be with my father, all the ill feeling seemed to melt away. It didn't matter where the fault had been historically – something had to give. Gerry was close to both Vilma and Donna and somehow she managed to clear the air between them. Without articulating why, years of tension were sorted, and to everyone's relief, the past was forgotten. I can't help but think how sad it is that it took Dad's death to sort out so many years of unnecessary pain, but what a wonderful thing that something so positive came out of our loss.

That Saturday, Dad sat in the front room with his huge family, going through old photographs. Berni in particular loved looking through them and Amber and Toby learnt lots about their older brothers and sisters that they had never known. Dad kept falling asleep. On Sunday he got dressed and in the early afternoon we had family photographs taken in the garden – we knew it would be the last time. Even walking into the garden had exhausted him and he fell asleep in the front room. There were times we checked to see if he was still breathing.

Back at work on Monday morning I was worried and called Mum. She said Dad was very weak and I asked to speak to him. His voice was so frail and quiet. I asked if I should come down and he said that I should. I said I'd come over the next day but he urged me to come that day. Vilma and I drove down that afternoon and by Monday night the whole family had arrived. Dad had got into a bed downstairs, and soon he was drifting in and out of consciousness.

We all spent time sitting alone with him saying goodbye. When it came to my turn I didn't know what to say. I held his hand and no words came out. Eventually I told him I loved him. I'm not sure I'd done that since I was a child.

For two days and nights we waited. Despite it all, it was a strangely beautiful time, sociable, loving and intimate. There were more than twenty of us there, including close family friends, and other family friends kept popping in bringing food or just best wishes. We slept on the floors or sofas and ate in shifts. There was some terrible and hugely inappropriate humour and several 'false alarms' when we thought he was about to die – and then he didn't.

We had Dad's favourite music playing in the background and scented candles lit. The All Angels version of Robbie Williams's classic 'Angels' was playing gently when finally at 6.45 p.m. on Wednesday 4 July he died, in his own home, surrounded by his family.

At 7.30 p.m. or so I texted Marianna and told her – there were lots of people at work who were aware of what was going on and wanted to know what was happening. Just after eight Gordon called – he said how sorry he was and I knew he meant it. He asked me to let Mum know he'd called and I did. She was really moved.

That evening we had a party. People kept arriving and bringing drink and it would have been rude not to have invited them in. Dad was taken by the funeral directors at about 10 p.m. and my brother Tim considered, but thankfully decided against, playing 'The Final Countdown' as he went. It was his current ringtone.

Two days later, on Friday morning, Gerry told a few of us that she was pregnant, but she wanted to keep it quiet for a few days. For Vilma and me this was bittersweet. We were obviously pleased for Gerry and Franki but the next morning we were due to do our own post-IVF pregnancy test. Nobody knew.

Early the next morning Vilma took the test. It was a really tense few minutes as we waited: a negative test was too terrible to contemplate. Vilma couldn't look, but slowly a blue line appeared in the second window – it was positive. So, three days after Dad died, he and Mum had two more grandchildren on the way. You couldn't make it up! In fact, as Shelly, Phil's partner, was already six months pregnant, the year ahead suddenly looked positively productive.

The funeral was booked for over a week later, on Friday 13 July. For the first time in many years I put my job second and decided not to go back to work until after it had taken place. Tim and I stayed with Mum and it was actually a really good week as the family planned the ceremony and talked about Dad. We all contributed to the planning, although as the week progressed it became clear just how much Dad and Tim had planned the readings, hymns and so on before he died. In fact Tim choreographed an incredible funeral – Dad would have been so proud, as I know Mum was.

The night before the funeral was the Labour Party's biggest ever fundraiser. It was held at Wembley Stadium and was a sports-themed dinner. It had been months in the planning, and I made sure that I received regular reports of how it was going from Carol Linforth, who had done an incredible job organising the event.

My job at the funeral was to deliver a eulogy. I spent the whole week writing it, clearing it with Mum and my brothers and sisters and practising reading it without crying. Dad's children carried the coffin in and out of St Mary's Catholic Church, where we had all grown up. The church was packed with more than 500 people from every aspect of Dad's life and I delivered the hardest speech I had ever had to give:

> In the end, nothing we do or say in this lifetime will matter as much as the way we have loved one another.

For just over sixty-two years, Dad, David, lived life to the full and has left a positive mark on many, many lives. Today we celebrate that life.

Dad was born just outside York in 1945, the youngest of eight children in a close Catholic family. As the youngest the others thought that he was a bit spoilt. At the age of eleven he left home to train to be a priest. He was there for over six years and just before he was due to take his A-levels, aged 17½, he decided that the priesthood was not for him.

On behalf of myself and my brothers and sisters, I have to say that we are very glad that he made this decision.

Leaving the seminary was a traumatic experience, and it would be fair to say that Dad's decision was not sensitively handled. He was woken at 6 a.m. and taken to the train station, and told that he was 'a bad apple in the barrel'. How wrong they were.

This, plus the death of his brother Peter a couple of years later, had a profound effect on Dad that lasted until he died. Ultimately it strengthened his faith, but it also made him strive to succeed and probably a bit stubborn. Mum's nickname for Dad was 'Victor Meldrew', and we knew what she meant.

For a few years after leaving the seminary he had a 'wild period' where his parents became worried about his drinking – ironically, something that Dad has worried about with all of us as each of us has gone through our own wild periods.

Dad then made the decision that was to set the course of the rest of his life. He began to train as a psychiatric nurse. Whilst training he met another student nurse – the woman he loved until the day he died – our mum. They married in early 1969, and I was born a few months later. I stress a few months, as aged about twelve, I realised to my horror the full implications of what I had hitherto assumed was a short pregnancy.

Dad was promoted and then promoted again and the family expanded. We moved to Poole and again the family expanded – and to be honest it has been expanding ever since.

He loved working for the NHS and Poole Hospital in particular. He also loved being a foster carer, loving the children who joined our family as if they were his own.

The whole of my life, and my brothers' and sisters' lives, has been dominated by my parents' partnership. It has nurtured, protected and grown every one of us. They struggled and overcame financial hardship, they supported each other through the death of our brother David, who passed away shortly before he was born, and they taught us the value of love, support and caring for others.

As foster carers, as parents, as friends, as grandparents, they changed lives for the better. Dad was committed to and actively involved in so many things: education, social services, foster care, the Church, the health service, the Labour Party and his family.

In each area his attitude was the same: valuing others, making sure that no one was left out and that no one was left behind.

And then our healthy, young-looking, marathon-running dad became ill with cancer of the shoulder and had major surgery. To be honest he never fully recovered. He had to take early retirement and then needed major surgery again. Cruelly, he seemed to recover and then last year began a succession of illnesses that culminated in the cancer of the kidney that ultimately killed him.

I am pleased to say that despite his illness he never once lost his favourite obsessions – in particular sweeping, cleaning and emptying the bins. He also never lost his sense of humour – even if it was occasionally a little quirky. I remember a few weeks ago when he was sitting in the kitchen at home watching TV, near the boiler. The boiler was throwing out some heat and Dad seemed a bit hot. One of us noticed that he looked uncomfortable and said to him, 'Dad, why don't you move? It will kill you sitting there.'

Quick as a flash Dad said, 'Don't worry, it's not the heat that will kill me, it's the cancer.'

For many years Dad had been thinking about whether to apply to become a deacon. Last year he finally started his training and found the spiritual journey that he undertook a challenging and rewarding experience that strengthened his faith.

Occasionally throughout his subsequent illness his faith was inevitably challenged, but to the end he found his deaconate training a source of enormous personal strength and faith, and he died with his faith stronger than ever, in no small part thanks to the deaconate course.

When Dad died, he died with his family around him – we were all there. We sat with him for nearly forty-eight hours.

The night before he died was full of tears, but also some typical Watt family humour and an awful lot of laughter. Dad, despite being semi-conscious, smiled at some of the jokes.

Friends popped in and out and children were playing. Yes, we cried, but we also supported each other. It was a desperately sad experience – but also strangely uplifting. It was definitely a relief – none of us wanted Dad to suffer any more.

And that I think will be Dad's greatest legacy – he and Mum taught us the value of family, the value of community and valuing others and the value of inclusivity. That legacy will live on in every one of his children and grandchildren.

Mum: Dad said that he had the easy bit – he just had to die. You have to cope with his death and keep living. He was right. I know that you are proud of each of us. We are more proud of you. You have more lives to change for the better, work still to do – and each of us will be there for you.

In the end, nothing we do or say in this lifetime will matter as much as the way we have loved one another.

David, husband, colleague, friend, granddad – Dad – this part of your journey is over. We love you. Sleep well. You deserve it.

# 10. ROUGH TRANSITION

I was on a junket in Strasbourg when Gordon decided to launch his latest grenade. I had flown there to meet Labour MEPs, something I tried to do a couple of times a year to catch up with what they were up to and make sure they knew we hadn't forgotten them. Normally, we'd meet in Brussels, and I was excited to be in a different city.

I dropped my stuff off at my hotel, wandered round town a bit, then hooked up with Gary Titley, the leader of the Labour group at the European Parliament, and a few other MEPs. We had a great evening – although the French aren't big on vegetarian food the wine more than made up for it. But while I was having fun on the Continent, trouble was brewing back home.

It was September 2006, and Gordon was restless. For weeks, there had been rumours that he was plotting an attempt to unseat Tony after tiring of the Prime Minister's persistent refusal to say when he was planning to stand down. The Chancellor had been working himself up about it for a very long time now and was finding it increasingly difficult to hide his impatience.

Of course, tensions over when Gordon would become Prime Minister had been simmering for years. The Chancellor's hopes that Tony would finally come good on the legendary 1994 deal they made as they dined alone in the Islington restaurant Granita were repeatedly raised, then dashed. On many occasions, the keys to No. 10 came tantalisingly within Gordon's reach, as Tony wobbled over the strain the job was putting on his family and the ferocious public backlash over the Iraq War. Whenever Tony's popularity in the country waned, Gordon's stock among Labour MPs and activists would rise, and he would become more aggressive in his demands for Tony to set out a timetable for departure.

The summer of 2006, however, was particularly febrile. Labour MPs were furious at Tony's stance over the war that had broken out between Lebanon and Israel in July, after Hezbollah militants fired rockets at Israeli border towns as a diversion for an anti-missile attack on two armoured Humvees patrolling the Israeli side of the border fence. Ten Israelis were killed in the incident and the clashes that followed, and Israel retaliated and began bombarding Lebanon with massive airstrikes and artillery fire.

There is a very strong pro-Palestinian constituent in the Labour Party. This leads many to be instinctively anti-Israeli and, even though elements from within Lebanon started the war, they were furious at Tony's refusal to back international calls for a ceasefire. They hated the spectacle of their leader siding with George Bush and the Jewish state, when they believed it was the Lebanese, who had lost more than 1,000 lives, who were the real victims.

In early August, Ann Clwyd, the chairwoman of the parliamentary party, publicly warned that the 'vast majority' of Labour MPs disagreed with the government's strategy. Conditions were ripening for Gordon to strike.

No. 10 was painfully aware of the risk, and I'd talked to John McTernan, Ruth and Ben about how we might deal with a coup. The obvious danger zone was the party conference in Manchester in September and we thought we were ready for any stunt Gordon and his allies might pull.

But on 1 September, Tony gave an interview which lit the touch-paper, prompting those who wanted him out to act sooner than we'd anticipated. With hindsight, it was almost bound to blow up in his face, but he was fed up of being asked by journalists how long he planned to remain in office, and couldn't contain himself any longer. During the interview he not only for the umpteenth time refused to name a departure date, but also ruled out saying any more on the subject either before or during the party conference, which was due to open on the twenty-fourth. 'I have done what no other Prime Minister has done before me. I've said I'm not going to go on and on and on, and said I'll leave ample time for my successor. Now at some point, I think people have got to accept that as a reasonable proposition and let me get on with the job', he declared.

Gordon's supporters were incandescent. As far as they were concerned, Tony had metaphorically stuck two fingers up at them. That weekend rumours swirled that the Chancellor's allies were preparing to act.

I went to Strasbourg anyway – to be honest I thought we'd heard it all before. It was Monday 4 September. Returning from my dinner with Gary and the other MEPs, I turned on the satellite TV in my hotel room to hear reports on the BBC of a letter being drafted by a group of Labour MPs calling on Tony to go. I called Alicia and she confirmed that there were very strong rumours that something was being planned. I went to bed worried but still not quite believing that anything serious would happen.

Next morning, the momentum was building, with reports of another private letter, this time from two formerly ardent Blairite MPs, Siôn Simon and Chris Bryant, urging Tony to resign.

Downing Street despatched David Miliband, then environment secretary, and a staunch ally of Tony, to try to defuse the crisis by signalling that the PM would go quietly 'within twelve months'. The damage limitation strategy didn't work: MPs were now demanding a 'bankable' public statement from the Prime Minister himself. Suddenly it felt much more serious.

John Prescott was furious. I was sitting in Gary's office in the Strasbourg Parliament when he rang me on my mobile.

'Peter, it's John. What the hell is Gordon doing?' he demanded.

I shot a meaningful look at Gary and the others in his office. Clearly it was going to be a difficult call, and they left the room. JP was in a foul temper, not just at the behaviour of the rebels but also because he was out of the loop. He had a foot in both camps and liked to think he knew everything worth knowing. This had caught him by surprise. 'I understand why Gordon's pissed off, but this is not the way to go about things!' he fumed.

He quickly realised I didn't know anything more about it than he did, spluttered something about Gordon's disloyalty and hung up. While the media was never able to prove that Gordon was behind what was happening, it was obvious that JP had his own view of the matter.

The sense of panic in No. 10 was worsened by the leak of a highly embarrassing private memo setting out some options for Tony's exit strategy. It had been written months earlier, mostly by Ben Wegg-Prosser, but the timing could not have been worse. In cringeworthy detail, the secret draft outlined plans to treat him like a rock star, with appearances on prime TV and radio shows and a stage-managed farewell tour.

'He needs to go with the crowds wanting more. He should be the star who won't even play that last encore,' the memo gushed. To add to the misery, it speculated on Gordon's likely reaction, listing it under a section headed 'threats and opportunities'. 'The more successful we are, the more it will agitate and possibly destabilise him,' it said, blowing a hole in the official line that relations between the Prime Minister and Chancellor were hunky dory.

That night, rumours began swirling that a minister's name was among those on the letters calling for Blair to quit. It was clear I needed to get back to London fast.

Back at Westminster on Wednesday morning, the rebellion was escalating, with news that Tom Watson, a junior defence minister known as a 'Brownite', was the member of the government who'd signed the letter calling for Tony to go. At 11.12 a.m., Tom resigned. Downing Street was under siege.

Unusually, the next day I had routine meetings scheduled with both Tony's and Gordon's teams, part of laying the ground for the transition of power. I also had separate meetings with Tony and Gordon themselves. I sat down with Spencer Livermore and Sue Nye at the Treasury just as Tom's resignation was confirmed and made some remark about all the drama. I felt I couldn't pretend everything was normal.

'I've no idea what you're talking about,' Spencer said, putting on his best poker face.

Just after 1 p.m. and I was still in the Treasury, this time sitting alone in Gordon's office waiting for him. He strolled in. 'What's the theme going to be for conference?' he asked me, as if nothing was happening.

'It's up to you and Tony,' I replied – obviously it wasn't my call.

Gordon scowled. 'You can never get a straight answer out of Tony,' he glowered.

By now, another junior member of the government, Khalid Mahmood, a parliamentary private secretary (PPS), had announced his resignation. No. 10 was desperately trying to stay afloat as David Cameron declared the government was 'in meltdown'. Rumours were swirling of more resignations to come.

'Obviously things are especially difficult at the moment,' I replied to Gordon, a huge understatement in the circumstances.

'These things will blow over,' he said dismissively, as if none of it really mattered.

'It's very unsettling for the staff,' I pointed out, really annoyed at how offhand he was being.

'It won't go on very long,' he replied, and the subject was closed, though he suggested coming over to see the staff at party headquarters – something he'd never done before. He was obviously keen to keep the party machine on side. I didn't respond to the suggestion, thinking it would be a bit weird if he just rocked up. It wasn't as if he made a habit of dropping in.

There was an agenda to go through, and for the rest of the meeting, I briefed Gordon on the state of the party's finances, delivering my usual grim message about how broke we were, and he gave me his usual platitudes about how it was all going to be okay.

At 2.01 p.m., four more PPSs – Wayne David, Ian Lucas, Mark Tami and David Wright – quit their jobs in protest at Tony staying on.

Given the unfolding crisis, I had fully expected my scheduled meeting with Tony to be cancelled and was surprised nobody had rung me to say it was off. I left the Treasury and made my way down King Charles Street and past the Foreign Office onto Whitehall. I headed through the back entrance to No. 10, where I found Ruth watching live reports of the resignations. She was typically pragmatic. In her view, Tony would survive but both he and Gordon would be damaged. Ruth was great at being absolutely to the point.

'Gordon is doing more to damage the party than anything else. No one will thank him for removing Tony even if he succeeds,' she said.

As I waited for Tony, I popped my head round the door of the office next door to Ruth where John McTernan was based. He and I sat for half an hour watching the rolling news. He said he had heard another two PPSs were ready to go, and that the rebels were spacing out the resignations for maximum impact. He was really angry, and we talked about how ridiculous it was for Gordon to be doing things in this way.

Vic Gould, Tony's PA, came to find me, saying Tony was ready to see me. I went into the his office just off the Cabinet room. He was standing up, looking the worst I'd ever seen him – old, grey and drained. He seemed sapped of all energy. 'Do you mind if I go out and have a wander round?' he said, gesturing towards the veranda.

I strolled out with him. 'Tony, I'm so sorry about what's happening to you. It's so wrong,' I said, meaning it wholeheartedly. After everything he'd done for the party, it seemed so unfair.

'It's just politics,' he said, doing his best to sound unfazed, though it was obvious he was shell shocked.

'Why is he doing this?' I asked, without actually mentioning Gordon's name.

'It's just Gordon. He can't stop himself. He always has to push, push, push,' Tony replied flatly. Like JP, he was in no doubt about the Chancellor's hand in the revolt.

'Let's be clear,' he said in a steely voice. 'If I thought for one minute that the party didn't want me to be leader, I would go. Maybe they do?'

I replied that as far as I was concerned, the party did not want him to go. 'Give me a couple of hours, and I will demonstrate to you that there is a strong will for you to stay,' I urged him.

We wrapped up, and I hurried back to the office to prepare a report for him to prove what I'd said. I called all the party's regional directors around the country, and asked them to take the pulse of the party. These were the crack troops of the party machine. They knew where the bodies were buried and who really mattered in their patch, and they were 100 per cent loyal. Soon the calls were flooding in. I could not find anyone who wanted Tony forced out like this. Indeed, the overwhelming feedback was anti-Gordon. As far as Labour staff and activists were concerned, the Chancellor had shot himself in the foot.

I also asked Marianna to get a report from Tracey Paul, who managed our call centre staff, about what party members and the public were saying when they called in or emailed us. The week before Gordon's move against Tony most people were calling for Tony to go – but things had changed. From the Monday, when reports emerged of a plot, we had been inundated with calls condemning Gordon and in favour of Tony.

I went back to No. 10 later that evening to deliver the report to Ruth. 'You can see for yourself how positive this feedback is. Make sure he knows there is a real strength of feeling that he should stay,' I told her.

All the same, by 10 p.m., seven PPSs had resigned, and it was obvious Tony was going to have to do something if he wanted Gordon to call off the dogs. The next day, in what was a big climbdown for him, he finally gave in to the Chancellor, and publicly confirmed what David Miliband had said the day before, that he would step down as Prime Minister within twelve months. It was the 'bankable' public statement Gordon's henchmen wanted. The Labour conference in two weeks' time would be his last as Labour leader, he announced – though he still did not give a precise date for his departure. He also apologised for the spectacle we had made of ourselves as a party, admitting, 'It has not been our finest hour, to be frank.'

Gordon had finally got his way – but there was still plenty of time for more rows before Tony left.

# 11. SMILES AND HANDSHAKES

The drama of the coup was over, and I was looking forward to a relaxing weekend with Vilma. We had been invited to a party on Friday night and set off in good spirits. We were staying over at the hotel where the party was being held and I just wanted to forget about work for a bit.

It was a wedding anniversary party for a friend of Vilma's from university called Patricia and her husband Tunde. The party was lively but Vilma was really down. She says she was lonely, and I was really tired. We had gone along with Naomi, another of Vilma's friends, and her husband Oded, but instead of joining in properly, I spent most of time on the phone. Vilma was really angry and just got drunker and drunker, so I decided to call it a day and after just an hour at the party, I headed to bed. I was simply too exhausted to engage with anyone.

The following day we went with Naomi and Oded to Portobello Market. As we wandered among the stalls, my mobile rang. It was Gordon. He said he'd been thinking about the future of the party and how to strengthen it. 'I want to come and talk to all the staff on Monday,' he announced.

I was surprised. Though he'd mentioned the idea a few days earlier, I hadn't expected him to follow through. I rang Ruth. 'I don't know what he's playing at,' I said.

'Well, we can't exactly stop him doing it,' she replied, agreeing it was strange. 'Keep us posted.'

On Monday, someone from No. 11 rang to say Gordon couldn't make it after all but wanted to reschedule for a few days later. I was anxious about the visit. After the events of the previous week, I was worried the staff might be a bit frosty. There was a lot of loyalty towards Tony and a general feeling that Gordon had behaved very badly. I shared that feeling, but did not want Gordon to pick up on it. There was no point in making things more difficult, and we had to have a decent working relationship.

Thankfully, when he arrived, he gave a warm speech and was received politely. Everyone was sitting dutifully at their desks, and we laid on some drinks and nibbles in one of the media rooms, so he could meet a few people less formally.

It was all going quite well, until he decided to do a tour of the office. He wandered round the big open plan room with a weird fixed grin on his face, shaking hands with the staff and saying 'Thanks for everything you do' over and again.

There was no variation and he never added any small talk. As he approached people's desks, they would stand up, accept the handshake and they would wait for him to say something else. Each time there was an excruciating moment while they waited for him to speak and he just stood there staring back at them, before moving on to the next person.

It was all very wooden and embarrassing, especially when he forgot who he'd met and ended up shaking some people's hands twice. They were forced to go through the whole ritual again, pretending they'd not met him just a few minutes before. I watched from the sidelines cringing.

I interpreted Gordon's visit as a sign that he was worried that the attempted coup by his supporters had upset the party machine and he realised he needed some good PR. He was right of course, but if anything, his strange manner as he toured the office increased the misgivings of those of us who were angry about what had happened and unsure that he would be a successful leader. The episode was a painful illustration of his lack of social skills. He seemed so stilted, with none of Tony's easy charm. By contrast, the Prime Minister was very skilled at making everyone who worked for the party, no matter how lowly their position, feel important. His office kept a diary of staff birthdays and he would sometimes catch people completely off guard by ringing to wish them happy birthday. As you can imagine, those people never forgot it and he won their enduring loyalty.

Three weeks later, at our annual conference, you could sense the backlash against Gordon over the coup. We were in Manchester, and everyone now knew it would be Tony's last conference as leader. While many in the party were glad and believed it was right that Gordon should take over soon, others were already feeling uneasy. I sensed a great deal of guilt about the way in which the Prime Minister was being harried out of office. It was a difficult conference for Gordon, whose keynote speech was totally overshadowed when a reporter overheard Cherie gasping 'That's a lie' as she listened to him heaping praise on her husband. Immediately afterwards, there was a big hullabaloo over whether she really said it, but she later admitted privately to me that she did. Gordon certainly wasn't feeling much love coming his way.

Meanwhile Tony delivered a sensational and highly emotional speech. It was one of his best ever, and he won over the audience within seconds by making a joke about Cherie and Gordon. 'At least I don't have to worry about her running off with the bloke next door,' he quipped, and everyone roared with laughter.

He admitted it was hard to let go, but said it was the right thing to do. 'The truth is, you can't go on forever,' he said. Many party activists were in tears as he told them, 'You are the future now.'

The speech wowed many of his fiercest detractors. As he left the stage and we all trooped out, there was a collective sense of 'Oh my God, what have we done?'

The next day, a leader in *The Sun* summed everything up. 'Has Labour gone stark staring mad?' it asked. 'It is hard to reach any other conclusion after seeing the party stand and cheer the most successful leader they've ever had – the man they've forced out of office.'

Many of the papers contrasted Tony's swansong with Gordon's speech twenty-four hours earlier, suggesting the Chancellor would have a hard time matching Tony's class act as Prime Minister.

There was a sort of collective grief among staff at that conference. Tony had dominated our professional lives for a decade and many of us felt we had grown up with him. It was hard to imagine working without him.

I wanted to do something to acknowledge how we were feeling, so I rang No. 10 and asked if they could give him half an hour to come to a small get-together with the staff the day after his speech. It was held in a private room in the conference hotel and almost everyone who worked for the party attended.

It was a very special and moving event. Among those present were staff who were about to leave because of the redundancy programme, and former employees who had recently left but returned to conference as volunteers. The room was packed, and when Tony walked in everyone went mad, cheering and whooping. He seemed quite embarrassed and gestured us all to quieten down.

'Thank you so much. It's nice to be among friends at last,' he quipped, one of his old conference jokes.

I gave a short speech off the cuff thanking him for everything he had done, and also for everything he would do over the next few months. 'You've not gone yet,' I teased.

I felt quite emotional, as did others. Some were dabbing their eyes. Tony also had a lump in his throat. He said that it was the first time it had really sunk in that he was leaving. He said his public appearances at conference that week had all been part of the job, a bit of an act, but now it felt very real. He thanked us all for our support, then went round the room thanking everyone personally. We all had photos taken with him.

However sad we felt, though, the deed was done – he was leaving in less than a year and we all had to make the best of it.

After the party conference, we began the groundwork for the transition and deputy leadership contest that would take place because JP was to leave at the same time as Tony. Despite the fanfare about his departure at conference, Tony still seemed to be in some denial. Shortly after the coup, *The Sun* had reported that Tony would leave office on 31 May 2007, but actually the date was totally up in the air.

From my point of view as General Secretary of the party, the critical point was that he left when he wanted to leave. That seemed to me in his best interests, and in the best interests of the party and the country. However, having made his big commitment to quit within a year, he did not seem to want to talk about it any further, and certainly wasn't offering up specific dates. I know he discussed it quietly with Ruth and Ben, but he was not at all keen to set the wheels in motion.

This was a problem for me, because quite reasonably, the NEC wanted to discuss the arrangements for his departure and the handover to Gordon, assuming nobody challenged the Chancellor for the leadership, another uncertainty.

Over the summer, there had been mounting pressure on David Miliband to consider throwing his hat into the ring, and there were rumours that he had quietly been canvassing support. I know of at least one Cabinet minister who he approached and sounded out, and this individual was not one of his confidants so there were no doubt approaches to others. Though he had not impressed at conference, which cost him momentum, we certainly could not afford to assume that he would not put himself forward, triggering a full leadership contest, and others might yet enter the fray. We needed to be ready.

Tony was adamant that he did not want any of this discussed at NEC meetings. He feared that as soon as anyone found out the NEC was discussing the logistics of his departure and the deputy leadership contest, the starting gun would be fired and his premiership would be fatally weakened.

However, I was under pressure to get things moving. In October, I told him I wanted to present a paper to the NEC meeting the following month, explaining that I was going to start looking at the practicalities of the transition. It would be the first formal acknowledgement in the party that there was going to be change of leadership.

Tony was not happy at all, arguing that it would undermine him as leader, and point blank refused to let me. No. 11 was equally concerned, fearing that the sooner we started the official transition process, the more time there would be for potential rivals to Gordon to come out of the woodwork.

I was not going to back down without a fight. My feeling was that if we did nothing, the dam would burst and we risked losing control. Everyone knew Tony was going in 2007 and if people were going to run against Gordon, they would anyway, so we might as well try to control the process. I devised a compromise to get Tony on board, suggesting that my presentation to the NEC would simply acknowledge what was ahead and defer a full discussion about it until the first NEC meeting in the New Year. I discussed this with Ruth and she arranged for Tony to call me direct.

I was at home in our bedroom, the quietest room in the house, when he called. He went through the usual small talk, asking about the family and so on, before letting me put my case.

'I'll keep the presentation very brief and simple,' I promised, explaining my plan.

'Isn't the reality that once we start officially talking about it, the contest will have already begun?' he said, sounding worried. I understood where he was coming from – after all, once official discussions about his departure started, it was not a great leap for people to start asking why he was sticking around. He felt the process could lead to demands for him to go right away.

'Yes, that's a risk, but I think there's an equal risk to doing nothing at all. We have to acknowledge that this is coming up, to make sure we control how it happens,' I replied.

'Okay, I'm trusting you on this one, Peter,' he said, not sounding very happy, and hung up.

Ruth had been listening in to the call and phoned me back later to say well done. I presented my paper as agreed and it bought us a couple of months before we began discussing it seriously in the New Year.

Through winter 2006 and in the early months of 2007, JP was privately pushing very hard for Tony to go in the spring. I don't think he really trusted the Prime Minister to leave – not unreasonably, as Tony had changed his mind so many times over the years about what he wanted to do. However, we at party HQ knew this really was it, and I didn't see any point in forcing him to go a month or two before he wanted.

The Treasury was not keen on a spring handover either – it would have meant Gordon would be leader for the local elections, and he wasn't exactly jumping at that prospect because he knew we would be hammered. In February 2006, the Chancellor was badly burned in a by-election right on his doorstep in Dunfermline & West Fife following the death of the MP Rachel Squire. It was one of Labour's safest heartland seats, with an 11,500 majority, and though we anticipated that the majority would narrow a little, nobody thought the seat was at risk. In an unprecedented move, Gordon declared he wanted to be in charge of the campaign. I'm sure he thought he could ride in on his political white charger and deliver a dazzling result, but the outcome was actually a shock defeat to the Lib Dems. The experience must have been very bruising for the Chancellor, who had been so personally involved, and he was in no hurry to repeat it.

There was a lot of hand-wringing about the by-election result, and the media questioned how Gordon would go down as leader in the leafy suburbs of Essex or Surrey if he could not hold onto a traditional Labour seat on his own doorstep. The defeat fuelled speculation that someone might run against him for the leadership and made the Treasury very nervous of taking over before they were absolutely ready. Behind the scenes, May or June was firming up as the likely time of the handover.

One of our most important tasks was to thrash out rules for the leadership and deputy leadership contests. Though it was not clear whether anyone would emerge to pose a really serious challenge to the Chancellor, the veteran left-wing MP John McDonnell had made it clear he hoped to run, so there would definitely be a contest of some description. We expected at least six runners for the deputy role, so it would be a proper competition which would require careful organisation.

We were under enormous pressure from MPs and figures on the NEC to devise watertight rules on donations to the campaigns. It was important that there should be guidelines for the candidates about how much they could spend and how the money should be declared. However, it was a difficult balancing act. I was conscious of the potential consequences if the winner was found to have breached the regulations sometime after the event. We could not afford to find ourselves in a position where there were calls for the new incumbent to quit. The NEC was very keen that we set a cap on spending but I argued against it. I was concerned that if there were a really tight contest between Gordon and another candidate, and we later discovered the victor had overspent, we would be in a very awkward position. The Treasury agreed. They knew that if Gordon did end up facing a serious challenge, he could easily raise another £50,000 or so to help fight off the rival. It was not in their interests to be restricted.

There was a huge amount of to-ing and fro-ing between myself, the NEC and the Treasury during this period as we all tried to agree the rules. Not surprisingly, Gordon took a keen personal interest. He was desperate to block any competition for the job he had long coveted. As Alan Johnson had bombed at conference, David was seen as his only serious rival. It was common currency at Westminster that Tony wanted the young environment secretary to run, and David hadn't categorically ruled himself out. However, he wasn't doing much to encourage the idea either, and as time went by it looked less likely. That didn't stop Gordon worrying. He was so fearful about facing a challenge that he actually wanted us to use our leverage to help lock him in as the only candidate.

Whatever he said in public (which was that he would 'welcome' a proper contest), the reality was that he was determined to torpedo possible opponents. My colleagues and I were shocked when, during the long negotiations about how the contest would work, he blatantly tried to skew the process as it was being drafted to make it more difficult for anyone else to run.

One of our plans was to have complete transparency over nominations for the leadership. The idea was that there would be a two- or three-day period in which MPs could nominate candidates, and during this time we would publish the names of runners and their backers as they came in. We knew that many MPs who were potentially interested in supporting someone other than the Chancellor would sit on their hands and wait to see which way the wind was blowing, and we felt it was important that everything was open. However, Gordon did not want us to publish the names of any candidate until they had at least forty-five nominations, the minimum required to run. This would have made it very difficult for anyone but him to stand. If we had bowed to his demands, it would have meant that MPs thinking about supporting someone else, like David, would have been left in the dark about the strength of the opposing candidate. Gordon, who wasn't going to have any difficulty drumming up forty-five supporters, would become an official candidate within minutes of nominations officially opening, with the list of his backers on the website getting longer by the minute. As an MP with an eye on your career, how could you risk not adding your name, when you had no idea if any rival was near to getting the forty-five required? Gordon's plan would have made it virtually impossible for anyone else to stand, and any notion of party democracy would have gone out of the window.

I was outraged by the proposal, which I saw as a blatant attempt by the Chancellor to sew up the contest, and went to talk to Mike Griffiths, who was NEC chair at the time. 'Gordon's asked us not to publish any names until candidates have all forty-five nominations they need. I'm digging my heels in on this one,' I told him.

Mike was dumbfounded. 'That's ridiculous!' he agreed, shocked. Others at HQ felt the same, and Gordon was forced to back down. I think even his own team realised it was madness.

In the event, David did not stand anyway, and John McDonnell failed to get forty-five nominations. To the disappointment of those who were unsure Gordon was the right person for the job and wanted to see him prove himself against a rival (not least because it would have seemed more democratic and we would have avoided accusations of a 'coronation'), he would be crowned leader without having to fight for the position.

I had been in two minds over whether the interests of the party would best be served by a contest. It was very hard to read how it would have panned out if one or more Cabinet ministers had thrown their hat into the ring. It could have become quite bitter and messy, and despite instinctively thinking nobody should become Prime Minister without some competition, I did prevaricate over whether a contest would be for the best. With hindsight, I think it was a terrible mistake that nobody else ran, but I understand why it didn't happen. Privately, it was quite clear to any Cabinet minister considering challenging Gordon that they would never be forgiven. They knew they would have no chance of being brought back into the fold if, as seemed almost certain, the Chancellor won. Whether you liked him or not, Gordon was a towering figure and it was not fashionable at that time to voice any doubts about his suitability for the job. You cannot blame people like David for baulking at the prospect of consigning themselves to the political wilderness.

Under the circumstances, Gordon's 'campaign' was not half as slick as it ought to have been. You would have thought that with so long to prepare, he and his team would have had everything ready for the official launch. They knew that even if there was no contest, they would have to go through the motions of presenting a manifesto, with campaign logos and so on. Yet with just days to go before the press event, scheduled for Friday 11 May, they still did not even have either a manifesto or any campaign materials. On the Tuesday, I got a call from Spencer asking us to bail them out.

Strictly speaking, it was not fair that Gordon should have any extra help from the party machine, but as no rival candidates had emerged we took a pragmatic view and decided to give him whatever back-up he needed. It would not have done us any good as a party if he'd looked like an idiot at his own launch. We also offered to lend his campaign team some technical equipment but they were quite sniffy, saying they wanted to try and keep some separation between his campaign and the Labour Party machine. I agreed with this in principle, but my interest now was in protecting our electoral asset. We needed him to look as impressive as possible.

Almost inevitably, given the extent to which everything had been left to the last minute, there was a cock-up on the day. As he gave his speech at the launch, Gordon's face was half hidden by glass autocues, and he looked pretty silly on TV. At least it underlined his claim that he had 'never believed presentation is a substitute for policy' but his people were sheepish. Twenty-four hours later, I got a call from Spencer asking if we could provide more support for his events team after all.

Once it was clear the Chancellor would be the only leadership candidate, the onus was on making the deputy leadership contest as exciting as possible. At this stage the NEC had agreed an official 'line' about the deputy leadership contest, which was that there wasn't one taking place. The party's public position was that there was no vacancy to fill since Tony had yet to say exactly when he was going, and until Tony left, JP was staying put.

We had agreed to hold this line until the date of Tony's departure was fixed. The leadership and deputy leadership contests would not begin before then. However, behind the scenes, preparations were under way. Six candidates were expected: Harriet Harman, Alan Johnson, Hilary Benn, Hazel Blears, Jon Cruddas and Peter Hain. In February, Jacqui Smith, then chief whip, and I began holding informal meetings with each of the declared deputy leadership candidates every three weeks to discuss the ground rules, official and unofficial, for the contest. The idea was to try to nip any problems in the bud, such as the paranoia among the candidates that Hazel, as party chair, would have some unfair advantage. The other candidates wrongly assumed she would have access to party databases and other valuable information about Labour members, and it took a lot to convince them otherwise. She was in a very awkward position. As party chair, she could not really go against the NEC 'line' about there being no contest and announce her intention to stand.

They were strange events. I was amused to note that Harriet always commandeered the big armchair in Jacqui's office, while everyone else contented themselves with the smaller seats. She would pontificate about how she was going to be very ethical about the way she ran her campaign, only fundraising from small donors. She had been working very hard for months. I thought it was all absolute tosh and Jacqui and I would glance at each other, discreetly rolling our eyes.

There was a code of conduct for the candidates that they should not attack each other in the media, but they didn't always adhere to it. Jon kept writing articles saying Hazel had an advantage. He was very funny about it – he liked her a lot and joked that by slagging her off he was getting lots of publicity so he didn't mind if he was breaking the rule about everyone being nice to each other.

Hilary was very straight during the meetings with Jacqui and me. Though he did not shine in the contest, he was always very gentlemanly and nobody had a bad word to say about him. Peter was a bit puffed up – he really believed he was going to win and, to be fair, he had worked very hard at it. If ever we were organising a regional conference or some other event outside London, it was always a nightmare to get any Cabinet ministers to come along, but Peter would be happy to oblige. Nobody else was prepared to take the train to some Godforsaken town in the middle of nowhere, but he was a banker. It was a private joke in the party that wherever two or more Labour people were gathered, Peter would either be there, or have sent his apologies. He had been grafting like this for at least two years.

Frankly, it was hard to see how we could get the public very interested in an internal debate about Gordon's future deputy. The successful candidate was not even going to be Deputy Prime Minister, just deputy leader of the party, and it all smacked of navel-gazing. All the same, we thought we could generate a bit of a buzz by holding some televised hustings, and got Polly Toynbee to chair the first one, in the Midlands. All the candidates were paranoid about their rivals having unfair advantages and there was a lot of fussing about who would sit where, who would speak first and last, and so on. On the day, all the candidates except Harriet spoke at a rostrum. Peter stood up and gave a very long pre-prepared speech which he had not timed. The bell rang before he finished and it was all rather embarrassing. I thought Harriet was far and away the best – she talked off the cuff, very fluently, and though she was absolutely shameless about dog-whistling to the left, it succeeded. She was the star that night.

The choreography of the special party conference we would hold in Manchester, at which Gordon would be crowned leader and the results of the deputy leadership would be announced, was endlessly agonised over. In general, the plan was for lots of rousing speeches, clapping, cheering and group singing. I was going to give a short speech, thanking JP for all he had done for the party, something I was proud to do. I was feeling particularly affectionate towards him, as he had been so kind and supportive to my family over Dad's illness, personally ringing my parents to say he was thinking of them. They didn't know him but loved the fact someone so important was telephoning with good wishes. Even though he could be a pain, I'd always liked him, and it meant a lot to me to give this farewell speech.

Gordon's coronation was scheduled for Sunday 24 June 2007. In the deputy leadership contest, Alan had been the clear favourite throughout, though Jon, who had promised to put the party back in touch with its working-class roots and had strong trade union support, was expected to give Alan a good run for his money. I spent the day before the ceremony supervising the electronic count, which was being held in a small and cluttered office in the east Midlands. I had deliberately kept the operation very tight and when the final result flashed up on the computer screen there were just four witnesses – myself, Roy and two officials from the independent scrutineer overseeing the process.

Harriet had won.

'Bloody hell! Shall we have a recount?' I joked to the others, who were as shocked as I was. Though Harriet herself never doubted her ability to win, she had so many detractors in the parliamentary party that none of us thought she could do it.

I had made it clear that I was not going to tell anyone the result until the official announcement on Sunday, because I was sure it would leak. But as I drove up to Manchester on the Saturday, Sue Nye, Gordon's senior adviser and trusted 'gatekeeper', called. 'Hi Peter, Gordon wants to know who's won,' she said.

'I can't say. I've told everybody that we're keeping it under wraps until tomorrow,' I replied. 'You know what will happen if I tell anyone – it will get out, and it'll spoil the announcement.'

Sue went away to explain to Gordon, but rang again a few minutes later. 'Gordon totally understands the situation, but says if he can get out of one of his meetings tonight and excuse himself for a quiet word with you, would you just tell him personally?'

I could hardly refuse – he was the Prime Minister designate, and in any case I trusted him to keep his word. So at 10.30 that night, as agreed with Sue, I went up to the huge hotel suite where he was staying in Manchester with Sarah and their boys, to give him the news. He was padding around the room in shirtsleeves and socks – he had been putting the finishing touches on his big speech the following day.

'Hi Peter, thanks for doing this,' he said, closing the door on the study where his advisers were tinkering with the draft. 'It's just between the two of us and Sarah,' he added, conspiratorially.

'Harriet won.'

There was no mistaking it – his face fell. There was a long pause. Then he put his hands on my shoulders, and said, 'It will be all right. We'll make it all right.'

It was obvious he was shocked, and not necessarily comfortable, with the result. I was surprised, as she was supposed to be his preferred candidate, but the truth is, I don't think anybody except Harriet herself, and perhaps Joan Ruddock MP, her biggest cheerleader, really thought she would win. Gordon obviously hadn't been expecting it either.

Over a quick glass of wine, I told him that we would need to do some work with the Parliamentary Labour Party, because Harriet hadn't done very well with the MPs, most of whom had backed other candidates. We needed them to throw their weight behind her. Then I made my excuses and left. As I headed off, I wished him luck in his big speech the next day and he put his arm around me in a kind of half-bear hug.

'It's going to be all right,' he said again, with boyish enthusiasm this time.

Next morning, around ten, Tony phoned me, all agog to know who'd won the deputy leadership.

'I can't tell you,' I said, teasing.

'Go on!' he coaxed.

'Oh okay. Harriet.'

There was a sharp intake of breath. 'Oh well. Oh well,' he said slowly, sounding heavily disappointed. Though he was too diplomatic to elaborate, his tone said it all. It was obvious this was not the result he wanted.

At the handover ceremony, all the deputy leadership candidates were asked to sit together in a room behind the stage until the winner was announced. They were under strict instructions not to leave the room. The only people who knew the result were myself, the three senior colleagues who'd witnessed the count, Gordon and Tony. All were sworn to secrecy. As I made my way to the room where the candidates were sitting, waiting for me to break the news, one of our senior press officers asked me who'd won.

'Not telling,' I grinned.

'Oh well, it's okay, because I know you wouldn't be smiling if Harriet had won,' he joked back. During the contest, there had been a lot of private banter about Harriet, with staff joking they'd resign if she won. She was certainly a controversial candidate.

The room where the candidates were waiting was full of artificial bonhomie when Mike and I arrived to deliver the results. When I started speaking, the atmosphere became very tense. I told them they would have ten minutes to themselves after I told them who'd won, before it was publicly announced.

'I'm going to give you a print-out of the voting numbers, so you can see exactly how you did,' I explained. 'Please try not to look too pleased or too sad when we go into the conference hall, or it will be obvious to everyone you already know the result. Can I just say, Well done, Harriet, congratulations! You are the new deputy leader.'

All the other candidates congratulated her warmly, gushing about how brilliant it was that she'd won, though of course none of them meant it. Alan must have been sick as a dog as the result was so close. In the final round, he'd scored 49.56 per cent of the votes to Harriet's 50.43 per cent. I am convinced that if he'd worked just a tiny bit harder he would easily have swung it, but he was just not hungry enough for the job. Poor Hazel had come last. She'd called herself the Marmite candidate, admitting you either loved her or hated her, and so it proved.

Each candidate had been told to prepare an acceptance speech that could be printed off for the media. We needed these a little in advance of the official announcement, so we could prepare the autocue. Everyone except Harriet had dutifully handed over their draft speeches. She had given hers to Joan Ruddock. A desperate search went out for Joan, but when someone eventually tracked her down, she no longer had it, and it was lost. With Tony and Gordon waiting in the wings, the entire conference was delayed as Harriet frantically rewrote her spiel in a side room. Gordon kept popping in, trying to encourage her along.

'Are you nearly there yet, Harriet?' he would ask, as she desperately scribbled away. Not surprisingly, when she finally took to the stage, her speech bore all the hallmarks of a very rushed job, but it didn't really matter.

Following the announcement of the deputy leadership result there was a short break, before the big handover ceremony from Tony to Gordon. You would not believe how much detailed preparation had gone into the precise choreography. The main sticking point was whether Tony would be on stage for the event, a question that had been endlessly disputed. It was like dealing with two children. Gordon would say Tony should only be there if he wanted to, while Tony would say he would only do it if Gordon wanted him to. This went on for months. A few days before the ceremony, Tony finally decided he was prepared to be on stage for the handover. That's when the argument became really heated. Gordon wanted Tony to rise, give a very short speech and then remain standing while we showed some video clips.

The film was going to be a kind of 'life and times of Gordon Brown', accompanied by rousing music to whip the audience up into a frenzy before the man himself appeared on stage. Gordon's idea was that Tony should hover around on the stage for a full six minutes while the film was screened and then, as it wrapped up, say something like 'Ladies and gentlemen, I give you your new Prime Minister, Gordon Brown.'

Tony wasn't having any of it. He didn't know what he was supposed to do while the film was playing and felt he'd look an idiot. Did Gordon honestly expect him just to stay standing at the lectern during the film, with a reverential expression on his face?

'I'm just not doing it,' he said, in a voice that meant his decision was final. On the day itself, the issue had still not been resolved. It was absolutely typical that even on this final and most important of occasions, there was one last stand-off between the two of them.

I was very twitchy about the whole thing – the ceremony was a big showpiece and the culmination of years of work on the transition behind the scenes. The last thing I wanted was some kind of cock-up. We were still hoping that Tony would stay on stage and announce Gordon's arrival, but just in case he refused, we used the time created by Harriet losing her speech to record a voiceover that could be used.

Sarah Brown had asked me to go and sit next to her and Neil Kinnock for the ceremony. I took this as a great compliment, feeling as if I was very publicly being brought into the 'family'. As I sat down, I still had no idea what Tony was going to do when the film of Gordon came on. To my horror, as the big screen lit up, he just walked off the stage. All I could think was, 'Oh my God – is he going to come back?' If he didn't reappear, we would just have to use the voiceover.

Thankfully, when the film finished he just sauntered back onto the stage, looking as if nothing had happened, announced Gordon's arrival, and the rest went smoothly.

Professionally, this was an amazing moment for me. I had set myself two big goals when I started the job, one of which was orchestrating a seamless transition from Tony to Gordon. I had just ticked this box. The deputy leadership contest had gone smoothly, and we'd made it as interesting as possible. Okay, Harriet had won and I wasn't her biggest fan, but hell, you couldn't have everything!

'Bloody hell. We did it,' I thought to myself. I was on a real high.

Tony was off, and there would be no more rows with Gordon. After years of having to deal with two bosses, one in the Treasury and one at No. 10, finally I would only have one person to answer to. The long war of attrition was over.

Early that evening, Gordon had a fancy champagne reception in Manchester, with various celebrities and high-rolling donors, although nobody from No. 10 went. It was held in an upstairs room at the conference venue. Despite the bubbly I didn't really enjoy it. I was too tired and just wanted to go home. It was a case of staying as short a time as I could get away with, for form's sake. The party was full of people I didn't know – the new 'in crowd' – and I felt a bit out of place.

To Gordon's annoyance, Tony wanted to do one last session of Prime Minister's Questions in the Commons before he went. He had it all planned – he wanted to give a little speech, say goodbye, take off his glasses with a flourish, and walk out of the chamber. If he was to get his way, it would mean that although Gordon was now leader of the Labour Party, he would have to wait until after PMQs the following Wednesday to become Prime Minister.

Gordon was furious. 'I'm the leader of the Labour Party on Sunday, and I'm Prime Minister on Monday,' he huffed. I could see why he was pissed off, but Tony was adamant. In the end, we persuaded Gordon that the few extra days before Tony left would give him time to plan his Cabinet.

On Wednesday 27 June, with the House of Commons chamber packed to the rafters, Tony did exactly what he'd planned. There was total silence as he delivered his last words from the dispatch box.

'I have never pretended to be a great House of Commons man, but I pay the House the greatest compliment I can by saying that, from first to last, I never stopped fearing it. The tingling apprehension that I felt at three minutes to twelve today I felt as much ten years ago, and every bit as acute. It is in that fear that the respect is contained.

'The second thing that I would like to say is about politics and to all my colleagues from different political parties. Some may belittle politics but we who are engaged in it know that it is where people stand tall. Although I know that it has many harsh contentions, it is still the arena that sets the heart beating a little faster. If it is, on occasions, the place of low skulduggery, it is more often the place for the pursuit of noble causes. I wish everyone, friend or foe, well. That is that. The end.'

With that, he whipped off his glasses, and to a standing ovation, headed out of the chamber to start a new life. Soon after, Gordon's team began arriving at No. 10.

We had suggested that they retain some people from Tony's team, at least for a few weeks, to make it all easier. It made sense for there to be some old hands around who could show Gordon's people the ropes. But Gordon wouldn't hear of it. As Tony walked out of the Commons, there was literally a mass exit of the entire No. 10 team. They trooped out through the Cabinet Office, dumping their security passes on the way, and the new lot walked in to a sea of empty desks. There was no handover at all. Such was the level of petty rivalry and lack of trust between the two most powerful politicians in the country.

But for now I didn't care – my job was done.

# 12. THE ELECTION THAT NEVER WAS

It was a summer of love for Gordon Brown, and I was beginning to think I had underestimated him. Like many of my colleagues, I had had deep misgivings about him becoming Prime Minister. Though there was no doubt he had a brilliant mind, he totally lacked leadership skills, preferring to shut himself away with a tight cabal of acolytes than try to motivate and inspire a wider circle of people. More worryingly, he seemed to struggle to relate to other people, showing none of Tony's easy charm and affability. It was as if he carried the weight of the world on his shoulders and couldn't be bothered to hide how he was feeling, unless it was very important that he made a good impression. Often, he was downright rude.

A small dinner party he and Sarah threw in their flat at Downing Street one Sunday evening illustrated the problem. It was an informal do, to which my wife Vilma and I were invited along with three other couples – the lobbyist Jon Mendelsohn and his wife Nicola; a bigshot Democrat fundraiser named Louis Susman, who was soon to become US ambassador in London, and his wife Marjorie; and another American couple.

Vilma was excited but nervous – she has a dim view of politicians generally, and was also worried about what to wear. However, we spent a happy afternoon in Kingston choosing her a lovely new dress and she started to look forward to it.

When we arrived at Gordon and Sarah's flat above No. 10 we were all ushered into the drawing room, and there was some stilted small talk over aperitifs on the sofas while Sarah pottered around getting the meal ready. Gordon quizzed the Americans about how we could make better use of the internet for party fundraising, one of his pet themes, and before too long we were called into the dining room.

While Sarah was in the kitchen, Gordon began showing people to their seats but was interrupted by the arrival of one of the No. 10 staff, saying he had an important phone call. He disappeared, leaving Vilma and two of the other guests seated, and the rest of us awkwardly milling about. When he failed to return after a few minutes we all started to feel a bit silly, so decided just to sit ourselves down.

When Gordon finally reappeared, he was aghast to find us all at the table. 'I didn't sit you all down!' he exclaimed angrily.

It was hugely embarrassing and some of the guests started mumbling about whether he wanted them to get up again.

'No, no, you might as well stay where you are,' he replied huffily, taking a pew at the end of the table. Then he swivelled in his chair, so that he almost had his back to everybody, and leaned his head on his arm. For the rest of the meal he was monosyllabic, sulking because he had lost control of the seating plan. The plates had not even been cleared when quite suddenly, without saying anything, he just got up and left. As Sarah had also disappeared by then, we all quite literally had to show ourselves out.

'He's bonkers,' Vilma whispered, as we trooped out. She was shocked and upset by his behaviour.

I wanted to disagree with her – after all, he was my political master. But she was right. The whole evening had been utterly bizarre.

The morning after the dinner party, Jon and I had arranged to meet with Louis at the Ritz for breakfast. We were going to talk about how he could help us access potential wealthy supportive expatriates in the States. Towards the end of the conversation the subject drifted into politics generally. Louis was actively involved in Barack Obama's campaign for the Democratic nomination and was confident that he could pull it off. I was sceptical, but luckily decided to keep my opinions to myself.

We then briefly talked about the UK political scene. I said that I was worried that Gordon was struggling to adjust to life in No. 10 and that he was still trying to run everything himself. Louis agreed and said that he really liked Gordon but that his political antennae were not always the best. However, I did my best to be positive. Gordon was Prime Minister now, and we all desperately wanted him to make a success of it.

In his first weeks in the job, he surprised everyone. A string of crises – an attempted car bombing at Glasgow airport just four days into his premiership, an outbreak of foot-and-mouth disease (later traced to a government-run laboratory in Surrey) and catastrophic floods across the country – enabled him to play the national statesman, heroically abandoning his Dorset holiday cottage to convene COBRA, the government's emergency committee, and rushing to the rescue of farmers and soggy residents of drenched villages.

When he wasn't playing the knight in shining armour, he was busying himself courting the right-wing media, ditching plans for a super-casino in Manchester, sounding tough about cannabis and promising to deport more foreign prisoners.

The nation swooned at his performance, while David Cameron's stock sank to an all-time low. After a disastrously timed visit to Rwanda when parts of his Oxfordshire constituency were under 5 feet of water, two by-election defeats in which his party came third, and an unseemly spate of Tory Party infighting over the future of grammar schools, the Right Honourable Member for washed-out Witney was being dubbed 'dead-in-the-water Dave'.

I remember watching Gordon outside Downing Street in July and suddenly thinking that he looked like the real deal. We all so badly wanted to believe he would be a great success. Now, despite all our fears, it looked like he was going to pull it off.

By mid-August, the so-called Brown bounce had accelerated into a massive 10-point lead over the Tories. It was our best poll rating since before the Iraq War and we were all thrilled. For the first time in ages, it looked like the future could be ours. People were beginning to talk about cashing in on our lead by holding an early election.

Organising elections was a key part of my job and I had spent a long time modelling how much the next general election would cost, drawing up projections for a range of scenarios, from a snap election soon after Gordon took over, to a poll in 2008, 2009, or the last possible date, summer 2010. In the 12–18 months before Gordon took over, I held regular meetings with the No. 11 team – usually Spencer, Sue and Jonathan Ashworth – in an attempt to hammer home just how broke we were. It was important that they fully understood our dire financial circumstances before Gordon arrived at No. 10 and got fancy ideas. It was not an easy task. After years of TB–GB warfare, Gordon's inner circle had pretty much convinced themselves that Tony was the devil incarnate, responsible for all the party's problems, and they seemed to think that as soon as the Chancellor took over, everything would be fine. It was an attitude that almost certainly emanated from Gordon himself, who seemed convinced all the party's financial ills were Tony's fault. He was sure that as soon as he got to No. 10 the money would start rolling in. 'It will all be fine once I take over – millions of pounds will come in,' he would say.

He believed Tony had given too much free rein to Michael Levy and blamed them both for the smell of corruption now surrounding our fundraising operation. I would always feel like rolling my eyes when he said this, because he was part of the problem himself. He seemed to find anything to do with fundraising quite distasteful and refused to go out of his way to thank our donors, which hardly encouraged them to dig deeper into their pockets. He actively avoided the annual dinners we held in their honour, only ever turning up briefly for the reception, and our donors were very lucky if they even got to meet him. It was fairly obvious he was embarrassed to be seen around them.

In some ways this was sensible – he recognised that the public did not like their Prime Minister hobnobbing with millionaires on yachts. On the other hand, small gestures – a hug, a handshake, a personal thank you or a note – made a big difference to the people who kept the party going financially, and I don't think Gordon quite got the balance right. He viewed dealing with the donors as dirty and dangerous work, and found it hard to hide it. As a result, many of our most important contributors felt he didn't care about them, and I suspect they were right. Gordon's attitude meant I had no reason to believe our financial situation was going to improve any time soon – and that clearly had implications for election timing.

One of the first things he did as Prime Minister was to appoint

Douglas Alexander, the international development secretary, as general election co-ordinator. In mid-July Douglas called me to say that there was going to be a political cabinet at Chequers and he wanted to be in a position to update everyone on the state of the party's campaigning machine. It was probably in better shape than he and Gordon thought. Gordon's acolytes had spent months telling colleagues that Tony had been running down the party's infrastructure when the opposite was true: despite staff cutbacks, we had quietly been investing in the machinery needed for a general election, upgrading our software and our operations for targeting marginal seats.

Douglas came over to HQ on Victoria Street and I sat with him in the boardroom, along with some colleagues from our election planning team, and told him about the work we had been doing. 'We are actually much more ready for an election than you realise,' I said.

I attended the political cabinet the following week, listening as Douglas trotted out the familiar spiel about the party machine having been run down, but he did go on to tell everyone that we weren't in too bad shape, and thanked me for my work.

Not long after, Gordon asked to see me personally to talk about the party, its finances and next steps. Our meeting was scheduled for 2.30 p.m. in Downing Street, and was due to last half an hour. In an early indication of his chaotic working style, it ran hopelessly over schedule, as Gordon became more and more engrossed in our discussion. We sat on the terrace outside the Cabinet room, and he called in his old friends Ronnie Cohen and Nigel Doughty to join us. In the end I didn't get out of there until 5 p.m. – whoever was organising his diary must have had a complete nightmare.

At that stage, it seemed that Gordon was just taking soundings about whether an early election would be practical and it was unclear how seriously he was considering it. But his decision to appoint Jon Mendelsohn to beef up our fundraising operation added to the sense that he was cranking up the machine. Like Michael, Jon was prepared to do the job for nothing, so long as he had a commitment from Gordon that he would be given full access to Cabinet ministers. He knew he could not do the job effectively without their support. However, Douglas was deeply suspicious of Jon's new role and seemed to regard him as a threat. He worked himself into a complete lather over Jon's job title, fretting that he would be undermined if the new position sounded too grand. It was clear that he didn't like the idea of Jon having too much access to Gordon and other important figures, and I spent three weeks soothing egos and negotiating Jon's title and remit with Douglas and No. 10. Douglas was on holiday with his wife and kids in the States at the time, and would be wandering round some theme park ringing me to tell me how unacceptable the latest proposed job title for Jon was. It was all a bit surreal.

As Gordon's political honeymoon continued that summer, speculation about an early election mounted. Reflected in actual voting across the country, our 10-point lead over the Tories could mean that we added more seats to the 66-seat majority Gordon inherited. It was obviously a tantalising prospect, and newspaper articles began to appear suggesting the PM could go to the country as soon as October.

I was excited, but felt I needed to sit down with him again to spell out, in words of one syllable, the absolutely parlous state of the party's finances, so he would know precisely what we would be getting ourselves into. Gordon's people agreed and in late August it was arranged that I would give a presentation on our financial situation in the Cabinet room to a group consisting of the Prime Minister, Jon, Douglas, Spencer, Fiona Gordon, Jonathan Ashworth, Sue Nye and the American political strategist Bob Shrum, who was working closely with Gordon at the time.

I didn't pull any punches at the meeting, telling them that for the last ten years, we had in every year bar one spent more money than we had raised. Year on year our debts had soared, to a staggering £30 million. I took them through how much a general election would cost, showing them some of my modelling and explaining that even to run a general election on two thirds the scale of previous polls we'd need to raise more money, pound for pound, than at any time in our history. Though it was a blunt message, it was not entirely a negative one: politically, going to the country early seemed smart, and despite our desperately straitened circumstances there would also be financial advantages.

'We are so broke that a general election in October actually makes sense,' I told the meeting. 'It will cost us £8 million, and we will have an "immediate ask" to donors, which will be quite appealing. The longer we leave it, the more money we'll have to raise.'

I had one other important message for Gordon. 'It doesn't matter to us when the election is. I understand you've got to keep your options open. But you must be clear about your decision. What you can't do is march us up to the top of the hill, then march us down again,' I told him.

Bob was excited, but Gordon became quite grumpy – perhaps he was suddenly thinking about it seriously for the first time and reflecting on how much was at stake. He wandered out onto the terrace with Bob and they chatted privately for a while. A few moments later, Bob reappeared.

'Well done, Peter, he needed to hear that,' he said. He was concerned that people around the PM were too reticent to tell him things they thought he might not like to hear. A few minutes later, Gordon came back in from the terrace. He thanked me and said he'd taken on board what I'd said and needed to think it over.

As August rolled into September, Gordon continued to mull it over. Douglas and I talked regularly. He would say that the Prime Minister hadn't made up his mind, but that we needed to continue the groundwork.

Discreetly, we began talking to suppliers and revving up our election software, using robo-diallers (automated telephone systems) and the super-sophisticated voter profiling system Mosaic to increase our information about voters in marginal seats. We researched all the legalities, mapped out how Gordon would tour the country, and began talking to the banks.

Meanwhile, behind the scenes, some of Gordon's closest aides were pressing him to go for it. I was startled when one day Douglas spelled out their rationale: 'The truth is, Peter, we have spent ten years working with this guy, and we don't actually like him. We have always thought that the longer the British public had to get to know him, the less they'd like him as well' – or words very similar to that. Spencer was in the room at the time and didn't demur.

Though Douglas said it with a smile on his face, the sentiment was repeated many times in discussions among senior Labour figures at the time including during briefings with Saatchi and Saatchi, the advertising agency we had appointed for the election, whenever it came. There was a widely held view that we had a real window of opportunity while the British public still liked Gordon. Nobody could quite believe that we were in a position to pitch him as a figure of strength and leadership, versus Cameron as a figure of weakness and drift. Everyone was getting excited.

On 13 September, No. 10 deliberately leaked the advert that Saatchis had presented in their pitch to win the general election account, a simple image of the PM looking serious and statesman-like, with the slogan 'Not Flash, Just Gordon'. Douglas put out a statement confirming that the advertising firm had been appointed and saying we were 'delighted to have them on board'. Naturally it stoked speculation that an announcement was imminent.

By mid-September, we had a full election-planning team up and running. Logistically, it would have been impossible to fight a successful campaign without many weeks of preparation before it was officially called: billboards had to be booked, advertising had to be created and agreed, materials for candidates had to be printed, and so on. I made this absolutely clear to Douglas. I was concerned that he was living in a bit of a fantasy world, imagining that we could somehow keep all this preparation completely secret. He seemed to think that we could build everything up and then click our fingers and suddenly stop it without any consequences. I warned him that as soon as we began cranking things up the money meter would start ticking, but he made it clear we should press on. The dogs of war were being readied, and across Whitehall it became almost received wisdom that a snap election was about to be called.

Labour HQ was a frenzy of activity – photographs were being taken of every single candidate, customised campaigning materials were being designed for every Labour MP and constituency, staff were being asked to clear their diaries, and we made preparations to draft in scores of former employees, special advisers and activists. The minute the election was called, we would lose the use of the Government Car Service, so we had limousines booked to ferry ministers around the country on official campaign visits. Our regional staff were on standby and were

holding daily planning meetings. All leave was cancelled and we had
calculated the cost of reimbursing staff who'd already booked expensive
foreign holidays. On the day the election was called every Labour MP
was to receive a starter pack containing details of how to obtain 200
personalised posters and 5,000 personalised introductory letters to
voters. I'd sorted out a temporary £500,000 overdraft facility with the
Co-operative Bank to get us off to a flying start and discussed financial
support from the trade unions.

Lest anyone think we were going out on a limb, I should stress that all
this was taking place with the full involvement of Douglas, Spencer and
other people in No. 10. Bob was talking to Deborah Mattinson, Gordon's
pollster, who was conducting twice-weekly polls to gauge how solid our
lead was, and feeding the results back to Gordon. Stan Greenberg, a
high-profile Democratic strategist who advised Tony, Bill Clinton and
Al Gore, came over from the States to join the team. There were lengthy
discussions about the exact timing of the election announcement, with
everyone eventually agreeing on Monday 8 October.

At our annual party conference at the end of September the talk was
of nothing else. Bilateral meetings were held with the trade unions to
firm up exactly how much they could give us for the campaign, with
Tony Woodley, the general secretary of Unite, acting as an unofficial
shop steward, drumming up support from the other unions.

In a normal election cycle, the trade unions have some ability to
get the people they want onto candidate shortlists, but a snap election
created a unique opportunity, massively increasing their potential
influence over who should be parachuted into safe seats. There
would be no time for the usual long-drawn-out selection process for
candidates, so emergency rules were being drawn up to enable the
party to impose candidates. No. 10 was busy compiling a list of the
Labour strongholds that would be up for grabs once the election was
called because of planned retirements and promotions to the House of
Lords and discussing names with us.

As you can imagine, there was a lot of horse trading with the unions
about who should be eligible for these highly prized constituencies
with huge Labour majorities. We needed their financial support and

their backing to get the emergency rule changes agreed quickly, so they were in a powerful position. The Transport and General Workers' Union (T&G) – one arm of Unite – made it clear they wanted Jack Dromey, their deputy general secretary, on the safe seat list, and one was identified for him at Wolverhampton North East, the constituency of Ken Purchase, who was retiring. I remember having a conversation with Gordon about it at the party conference. He told me privately that Woodley was organising the unions, revving them up for the election campaign, and that one of the people on the safe seat list was Jack. He didn't seem entirely comfortable with it, but indicated that it was nothing to do with him. We held a meeting of NEC officers, including Jack, at which I updated everyone on election planning progress. When I turned to the issue of the safe seat list, Jack diplomatically excused himself and left the room. Together with Amicus, their other arm, Unite promised to donate £2 million to the campaign.

Everyone at conference was fired up. Harriet confided that she'd told Gordon she thought it was the right thing to do; Philip Gould was saying, 'Do it now.' Gordon was asked about it in interviews, and repeatedly failed to rule it out – Westminster-speak for confirming it was very much on the cards. Many of our regional staff left conference early to return to their offices and get on with the planning. Everything was in place, with the media centre fully kitted out for satellite transmission of the big launch.

On Friday 28 September, the day after conference ended, everyone involved in the operation converged at Victoria Street, hugely excited. But there was one area of concern: the manifesto, which was Ed Miliband's responsibility. Douglas arrived at HQ very agitated about it.

'I can't believe Ed Miliband,' he complained. 'You'd imagine that after ten years of waiting for this, and ten years complaining about Tony, we would have some idea of what we are going to do, but we don't seem to have any policies. For God's sake, Harriet's helping write the manifesto!' It was the first serious indication of a recurrent theme of Gordon's premiership: everyone around him thought there was some big plan sitting in a bottom drawer somewhere, just ready to be pulled out when the moment came. In fact, there was nothing.

That weekend we sat over endless cups of coffee at Labour HQ, war gaming. We tried to put ourselves in Cameron's position and work out what he was likely to do to try to regain the initiative. It was the height of the property boom at the time, and inheritance tax was a huge running sore among middle-class voters. The number of people forced to pay it had more than doubled since 1997, and respected voices in our own party such as Stephen Byers were calling for it to be scrapped. All of us, Douglas included, thought the Tories would make some big announcement about it; it seemed a no-brainer.

We discussed three possible responses if we were right: to attack the Tories' pledge as irresponsible and unaffordable, shrug our shoulders and say we'd match it, or try and trump Cameron by announcing we'd go further and scrap the tax altogether.

That Sunday, Gordon gathered his closest aides for a summit meeting at Chequers: Sue, Spencer, Bob, Douglas and a few others. I was not invited, but received a call from Douglas on the Sunday to say we were still on. There was just one week to go.

The following day, Monday 1 October, the opening day of the Tory Party conference in Blackpool, George Osborne, the Shadow Chancellor, did exactly what we'd anticipated, and announced the Conservatives would raise the inheritance tax threshold to £1 million. The announcement electrified his party conference, drawing thunderous applause and earning the Tories huge plaudits in the press.

We ought to have been pleased that they had proven so predictable, but instead of taking the sting out of it as quickly as possible with a robust response, we did the worst thing possible: nothing. The sorry truth was that nobody could decide which of the three options we'd discussed to plump for, and so despite knowing full well the Tories would do what they did, we had absolutely no answer when they did it. It was pathetic, and devastating evidence of one of Gordon's gravest weaknesses – an inability to make big decisions.

To make matters worse, Gordon then unexpectedly visited Iraq to announce a cut in troop numbers by 1,000. This figure began to unravel almost immediately, as it included a reduction of 500 already announced, and the Tories branded the visit a cynical pre-election stunt. I cringed:

we were planning a snap election days later. At best it was ill thought out and clumsy; at worst the Tories were right – it was also cynical.

By midweek, the media was dominated by excitable reports of a Tory fightback. Our lead in the polls was narrowing, and Douglas was getting jittery. I think No. 10 had convinced themselves we were going to win this election by quite a margin, perhaps forgetting that the last general election, in 2005, had been quite close. A win was a win, but with our 10-point poll lead in August, and all the excitement of Gordon's so-called honeymoon, they'd been banking on much more than that.

To my disbelief, Douglas started asking if we could 'pause' the preparations. I told him that would be completely impossible – everything was booked: we were either on, or off. We had already spent £1.2 million. Somewhere lying in a huge mail depot were hundreds of sacks of personalised letters to voters in marginal seats – 1½ million envelopes – waiting to go. To hit the doormats on Monday 8th, the day of the big announcement, they had to be dispatched from the depot the following day.

While Douglas wobbled, at Labour HQ it was all go. I could not let the staff know that No. 10 was getting nervous. It would have caused huge confusion, potentially crippling the entire operation at a critical point.

Then on Thursday Cameron called our bluff. Capping a barnstorming week in Blackpool, which had seen the near evaporation of our poll lead, he made a spectacular keynote speech, demanding an end to the weeks of frenzied speculation about the election. In a make-or-break move, he took the extraordinary risk of addressing his troops for an hour without notes, daring Gordon to call an immediate election. 'So, Mr Brown, what's it to be?' he taunted. 'Why don't you go ahead and call that election? Let the people decide. Call that election. We will fight. Britain will win.'

His speech went down a storm and the press coverage was sensational. A panicky Gordon summoned Ed Miliband, Ed Balls, Spencer, Douglas, Sue and Deborah Mattinson, for a crisis meeting.

On Friday morning, Douglas called. 'Peter, Gordon's not going to do it,' he said quietly. He sounded gutted – there was a huge amount riding on it for him too, as he'd pushed for it so hard.

I was gutted myself but snapped into organisational mode. There was hardly any point arguing. 'When's he going to make an announcement?' I asked, not only because the staff needed to know, but also because speculation had reached such fever pitch that it was unsustainable. Gordon could not just pretend nothing had happened, and was obviously going to have to say something to the media.

'Tomorrow,' Douglas replied, adding that we couldn't allow any sense that things were winding down until the Prime Minister officially announced it was not happening, or the political fall-out would be even worse.

I was aghast. 'So I have to keep all these poor sods working fourteen hours a day, in the full knowledge that it's all off?' I asked, incredulous.

Douglas muttered something about there being no choice, and the conversation ended.

Only six of us at HQ – myself, Marianna, Roy, Alicia, Chris Lennie and Hilary Perrin, who managed our regional team – knew that Gordon had backed out, and for the rest of the morning, we kept up the pretence in front of the staff. My face was a mask as a retinue of Pickford vans arrived to drop off all the extra tables and chairs we would no longer need and an army of BT men descended on the office to install a load of extra phone lines I knew we would never use. The T&G's cheque for £1 million arrived, and I quietly put it in a drawer knowing I'd never cash it. Thanks to a fortuitous postal strike the previous day, we were spared the huge embarrassment of the 1½ million personalised letters to voters already being in the post.

Feeling sick with disappointment for everyone who had put in so much work, I maintained this hideous charade all morning, but there was only so far my conscience would allow me to go. The staff were so excited, and I knew that unless I came up with some ruse, many of them would work late into the night. There was no way I was going to stand by and let that happen so at 1 p.m., I called a meeting of all senior managers.

'Gordon hasn't made a final decision, but we'll know for sure by Monday,' I told them, hating myself for the lie. 'So I want everyone to let their hair down tonight, either as a thank you for the work you've done, or as one last chance to have a night off, before the campaign officially starts. I'm going to put a few hundred quid behind the bar in the Old Monk pub and I want everyone out of here by 5 p.m. I mean it – I want everyone in the bar. We're locking this place up for the night at 5 p.m. sharp.'

I'm happy to say that the trick worked and at 5 p.m., everyone piled out of our HQ and our Newcastle office and trooped down to the local boozer, chattering excitedly about whatever they were working on for the campaign. I think they had a great night, but I couldn't enjoy the evening myself, knowing they were about to find out that all their work had been a complete waste of time.

At tea time the following day, Gordon Brown made his announcement in a interview at Downing Street with the BBC's Andrew Marr. I listened open mouthed as he tried to pretend none of it had really happened.

'I had a responsibility to consider it,' he said casually, as if he'd spent half an hour toying with the idea before dismissing it.

After thousands of hours' work, £1.2 million spent and huge sacrifices by all the party's dedicated staff, all with his encouragement, he added insult to injury by suggesting he'd done us all some kind of favour. 'When you're Prime Minister you've got the power to make this decision; people come to you and say "You must consider it" and you've got to consider it, that's the only fair thing to do, because you've got to exercise power with responsibility,' he said.

As he spoke, the fleet of limousines ordered at No. 10's behest was aimlessly circling Parliament Square. Blissfully ignorant of all the drama, they had come to Victoria Street, as arranged, to be picked up by staff who would then collect ministers and whisk them off on the campaign trail. They were sent away on a pretext, to spare us the humiliation of anyone spotting them lined up outside our offices when Gordon finally called the game off.

And so concluded the most farcical episode of Gordon's administration. Like the summer of love in 1967, by autumn, it had all turned sour.

# 13. FALL GUY

I found out I was in deep shit about twenty-four hours before the rest of the nation heard. It was Thursday 22 November 2007, and I had been hearing rumours all week that there was a bad story brewing about some of our financial donors. It involved the associates of a millionaire property developer from the north-east named David Abrahams who were donors to the party. The *Mail on Sunday* was sniffing around.

To be honest I wasn't that bothered – our donors were always getting a kicking in the press. It annoyed me that they were given such a hard time. These were highly successful individuals who didn't need the hassle that went with giving us money. The vast majority supported us for genuinely altruistic reasons and I felt they deserved to be looked after.

David had been actively and publicly supporting the Labour Party since 2001, and I'd met him several times at various dinners and social events. Though I didn't know him well, I liked him. I remember being quite excited once when he sent me an invitation to attend a black tie do as his guest. I had never actually been to a black tie do before. Later, the papers would dig up a cheesy picture of us together at this event, me with my clip-on bow tie slightly askew.

David had always made it clear he didn't want to be a donor. Unusually for a high roller, he was a keen grassroots party activist and told us he did not want his wealth to affect his relationship with his local party colleagues. However, for years he had been organising donations from the directors of his company, Ray Ruddick and Janet Kidd, and from his solicitor, John McCarthy. He also organised donations from the wife of one of his employees, a woman named Janet Dunn. They all made donations to the Labour Party. There was never any great secret about this at HQ. David told me he used an accountant to 'legally gift' the money to his associates. He had apparently been advised that as long as his associates were UK residents, on an electoral roll and – however briefly – legal and rightful owners of the money they were donating, there was no problem. Every donation was reported to the Electoral Commission.

Over a five-year period, Kidd, Ruddick, Dunn and McCarthy collectively gave us a total of £600,000 – money that was gratefully received. Kidd also donated money to Harriet's deputy leadership campaign. Nobody at HQ ever really thought these donations were anything other than lawful.

I was heading home from work at about 7.30 p.m. when I got a call from Jane Hogarth, in our fundraising division, to say she'd bumped into David at an event. He'd told her that a Sunday newspaper had been trying to talk to Kidd and Ruddick about their donations and that he was worried about it.

My heart sank – I was tired and dispirited about the way things were going with the party, and I was supposed to be taking the next day off. A week earlier, Vilma had given me an ultimatum about my job, telling me I had to choose between work and our marriage, and I had promised her a really nice family day together. Already I could see it was going to be dominated by ridiculous phone calls.

Doing my best to hide my irritation, I rang David straight away and asked what the problem was. To my dismay he seemed to be in a complete panic, fretting about his privacy and his identity being 'unmasked'. I tried to calm him down, telling him it was probably best if he just acknowledged his role in organising the donations. After all, he'd done nothing wrong. However, he was adamant he did not want to talk to any journalists. I began to feel uneasy: what I'd thought was going to be just another knocking story about some of our donors – tiresome, but no big deal – had the makings of something more serious.

The following day, I discovered that David's associates, Ruddick in particular, were not behaving like proud Labour donors when approached by the newspaper's reporters. Ruddick was apparently mouthing off about politicians in general and saying he 'couldn't stand' Labour in particular. This was news to me, since I had understood all David's associates were enthusiastic supporters of the party.

I was becoming increasingly alarmed and rang Gerald Shamash to confirm our legal position. As I'd expected, his view was that as the donors were technically giving their own money, it should not be a problem.

That evening, Harriet rang me several times wanting updates. Obviously she had a very personal interest, having accepted money from Kidd herself. 'Peter, do we have a problem?' she asked.

'Well, it's going to be a difficult story, but we should be fine,' I replied, trying to appear relaxed. I told her what Gerald had said.

She sounded relieved and said that she was pleased that she wouldn't have to give the money back. However, Jack Dromey rang me spitting blood, demanding to know why he had never been told about David and his associates.

I was surprised and indignant at his attitude – it was not our practice and never had been to involve him in the minutiae of organising the donors. If anything he avoided donors at all costs. We did update him about new donors, but these particular individuals had been giving money to the party for years.

All the same, I sensed trouble. I had been involved in big political crises before, and had always felt everyone rallying round. During 'cash for honours,' it had been Team Labour against the world. This was different. With every call I took from Harriet and Jack, the atmosphere grew cooler. David's associates had been contributing since long before my time. Many people in the Labour Party knew about it. Yet I began to get a creeping sense that I was on my own.

In the old days under Tony, I could have called someone like Alastair Campbell, David Hill or Ben Wegg-Prosser to talk things over. However, these days there was nobody in No. 10 I knew well enough to turn to for advice. I was managing this crisis alone. I don't mind admitting I was frightened – Labour's high command was in panic, and I knew I would be no match for them on my own.

Back home in Chessington, I sat alone in the kitchen late into the night, going over and over the donor reports in my head. I slept poorly, waking on Saturday to more bad news: David had been trying to pretend to be someone else on the phone to reporters. Things were spiralling out of control.

As we waited for the story to break Harriet, Jack and I held a conference call. I suggested we issue a statement saying that these were 'permissible donations from permissible donors', a position I had confirmed as true with Gerald. However, I sensed I was being cut loose.

At 11.30 p.m. on Saturday, the first edition of the *Mail on Sunday* appeared online. The story was far worse than I'd feared. 'LABOUR'S THIRD LARGEST DONOR: HE LIVES IN A COUNCIL HOUSE, DRIVES A BEATEN-UP VAN – AND SAID HE KNEW NOTHING ABOUT THE £200,000 THE PARTY RECEIVED FROM HIM,' I read.

In excruciating detail, the story contrasted Ruddick's modest £12,000 semi, his 'battered Transit van' and downtrodden appearance in his 'paint-splattered fleece top' with his extraordinarily generous gifts to the Labour Party. Described in the paper as a 'jobbing builder', he was first quoted denying all knowledge of the donations, then suggesting he and Kidd might have been 'set up', before finally spitting, 'I've never voted in my life. I can't stand Labour.' Eight hours later he'd apparently changed his tune, admitting to making a single donation. To add to the sense of subterfuge David had referred all enquiries to his lawyer, who told the paper his client had not been given enough time to comment.

I sat on the kitchen worktop and fixed myself a Pisco and Coke, feeling sick to the pit of my stomach. Vilma is South American, and she introduced me to Pisco, a Chilean poison which does what the name suggests.

We needed a strategy for handling the furore, so I arranged a conference call with Harriet, Jack, Dianne Hayter (at the time the most senior official on the NEC) and Fiona Gordon.

Head fuzzy with the Pisco, I briefed everyone on the conversation I'd had with Gerald, reassuring them we were on solid legal ground.

I suggested we put out another statement saying we would refer the matter to the Electoral Commission ourselves, 'in the light of new information' – specifically that some of the donors were not Labour supporters. Harriet and Jack vetoed this and after a brief discussion I backed down.

By lunch time on Sunday the media was in full cry and I was wondering if I had been stupid. Though I was still in no doubt that the donations were lawful, what an idiot I had been not to see how a story could be written which might make the donations appear very differently from the account I had been given and on which I relied! A wave of nausea hit me, and I ran to the bathroom to be sick. As General Secretary, I had been massively loyal to colleagues in difficulty, protecting them on many occasions when I could have fatally damaged their careers, but it was already obvious they were not going to return the favour.

I stumbled out, mouth tasting of bile, and lay down on the bed fully clothed. As I was staring at the ceiling, head pounding, Gerald rang.

'Peter, I've been looking at the relevant piece of legislation again. I've just discovered an obscure clause regarding so-called "agency arrangements". It's possible the law has been broken,' he said quietly.

'What does that mean for me?' I whispered – but I already knew.

It meant not only that my career with the Labour Party was over, but also that I might well be arrested, could be charged, and could even end up in prison. It was all horribly familiar. We'd only just emerged from 'cash for honours'. How could we be in this situation again? Hands trembling, I phoned Harriet to break the news.

'I thought as much,' she said grimly. The day before, she'd asked Gerald for a copy of the relevant legislation and had been studying it herself.

'I don't know what I'm supposed to do, Harriet, but if I need to resign, I will,' I said flatly.

I rang Fiona, who suggested Gerald get a second opinion from a QC. He immediately contacted James Goudie, Gordon's favourite barrister, who promised to look at the legislation and meet everyone early the following day to talk it through.

I was not invited to the meeting and, crucially, nobody asked me for the facts, but soon enough I would discover Goudie's devastating verdict: we had certainly broken the law. It was in nobody's interests to broadcast the fact that Gordon's own counsel reached this conclusion, but a copy of his advice was later handed to me for my records.

That evening Murray Elder rang, asking me what was going on. 'You can't resign, Peter. You're a level head around here, and there aren't many,' he urged.

I had not told him about my predicament, so conversations were clearly taking place behind my back. That night I barely slept. I lay in the dark, adrenalin pumping as I thought about how I would survive if I ended up in prison. I'm nobody's idea of macho, and I didn't fancy my chances.

In the morning, I set off for the office feeling a condemned man. When I arrived, Dianne, Harriet and Jack were already locked in a meeting from which I was obviously excluded. What followed was a kangaroo court. I was summoned before them as Harriet went through the motions of asking for a brief version of events, but it was clear nobody was interested in a proper account of what had happened. I walked out of the room knowing the game was up.

A few minutes later, Fiona called and told me Gordon wanted to see me in No. 10. While I was en route, he changed his mind and I was summoned back to HQ. As I sat down at my desk Harriet, Jack, Gerald and Fiona emerged from the meeting room and trooped past me, not one of them looking my way.

A few minutes later, Dianne called me into the meeting room again and put her hands on my shoulders. 'This is the hardest thing I have ever had to do, but I am going to have to accept your resignation,' she said.

I now know that while I was en route to Downing Street, Gordon had called Dianne, saying I had to resign. Goudie's advice – issued without even talking to me – had sent No. 10 into a tailspin.

'We think you are about to be arrested,' Dianne said, adding that it would be 'easier' for everyone, including Vilma and my mother, if I quit. The pressure I was under suddenly increased dramatically.

While Dianne left me to my thoughts, Harriet sidled up to me and put her hands on my shoulders.

'*Courage*, Peter, *courage*,' she said in a weird French accent, rubbing my neck. 'What you need to understand is that nobody thinks your personal integrity has been impugned.' It still makes me wince.

The rest of the day passed drafting a resignation statement. Agreeing the wording was a farcical process, with Gerald shuttling up and down the office with the draft as Dianne and I haggled over who would say what. Though we were only a few feet from each other, we were now operating as if we were on different sides of a war. I called Victoria Phillips, a solicitor I knew, to help me negotiate my exit from eleven years of employment with the Labour Party. At the same time, she found me a criminal lawyer, Greg Powell, just in case the police were indeed called in, and I fixed a meeting with him later that night.

I had warned Vilma that morning that I was either going to be sacked or would have to resign but I don't think she believed it. She has a tendency to think I'm being melodramatic. Now I rang her to tell her she needed to pack some bags, get the kids into the car and head for my mother's house before the media descended. I told her I would not announce my resignation publicly till I knew she was on the road. She could tell from my voice that it was no time to argue.

Around 3 p.m., Gordon called. 'Peter, I'm so sorry this has happened. I can't tell you how sorry I am,' he said.

Not wanting to draw out the conversation, I mumbled something about him not needing to apologise.

'It's in the best interests of the party. We will look after you,' he promised, and hung up.

An hour or so later Vilma rang to say she and the kids had set off. My resignation statement was issued, Marianna quietly collected up my belongings, and I handed in my three prized passes, to Downing Street, Parliament and Labour HQ.

On the back steps of the office, Marianna and I hugged and cried. There was no sign yet of the taxi we had called to take me to meet Greg.

'Don't wait,' I told her, not wanting to drag out this unbearable goodbye. She turned and left.

For a moment, I was alone on the street, a physical and political outcast.

The taxi rolled up. It was time to see my criminal lawyer. I was going to need him. For though the police weren't involved at this stage, thanks to the Prime Minister, who had just promised to look after me, they soon would be.

# 14. END GAME

My family was bombing down the M3 in our battered grey people carrier following the announcement of my resignation. They were on the run from the media, and I was on my way to see a criminal lawyer.

I felt many different emotions as I prepared to leave Labour Party HQ, but anger was not one of them, until I was shown the comment Dianne had tacked onto my resignation statement. I only saw it by chance as I was gathering up my belongings. Almost as an afterthought, my lawyer asked for a copy of the press release for her files. I scanned it for the warm words and expressions of regret that employers traditionally attach to such announcements and saw that instead, Dianne had stuck the knife in.

Her short but brutal statement claimed the party was 'shocked and disappointed to learn of the circumstances surrounding these donations' and emphasised that I had accepted 'full responsibility'. Under the circumstances, I wasn't exactly expecting a medal, but these words were calculated to blacken my name, suggesting I had knowingly set up some kind of secret operation.

In fact, David's associates had begun donating money to Labour years before I became General Secretary, and many senior figures in the party knew about the gifts. Due diligence had been shown. As Dianne knew full well, in resigning I was taking one for the team.

For a moment, I felt furious at the injustice of it all, but longer lasting was a most painful sense of betrayal. It was a feeling that would grow in the months that followed, and two years on, it has not entirely faded.

My taxi pulled away from the back of HQ, picking its way through the early rush hour traffic to the offices of Victoria Phillips, my solicitor, where I was to meet my criminal lawyer, Greg Powell. I was frightened. Though I was sure I had not broken the law, my experience during the criminal investigation over 'cash for honours' had taught me that laws can be interpreted in different ways. I knew it was only a matter of time before the police were called in.

I sat waiting for Greg in a room decorated in soothing pastel shades and remembered reading somewhere that prison cells were painted in these colours to calm inmates.

I was ushered into Victoria's office where I met Greg, who whipped out a legal notebook and began taking details. It was a strange moment, both disconcerting and reassuring: suddenly I was a proper case. He had a copy of the legislation relating to donations to political parties on his desk, and was the first person to take a statement from me.

'I'm not sure what law you've broken,' he said finally, when he'd heard my account. He sounded a bit exasperated. I think he was frustrated that I'd resigned. When I'd spoken to him briefly earlier in the day, he had urged me not to do so until he'd had a chance to look at the law and reflect on my position.

We agreed to meet the following morning to draft a statement to the Electoral Commission, saying that as far as I was concerned, I had acted with due diligence and met the party's reporting obligations. We arranged to deliver it in person as soon as it was ready.

By now it was past 8 p.m., and there was nothing more I could do except head home and try to get some rest. I was going to join Vilma and the kids at Mum's house in Poole, which we hoped would be a refuge from the media. I headed for Waterloo station barely able to believe the events of the day.

On the train, I finally had a moment to look at my phone, which had been silently flashing all day with calls and voicemails. I began scrolling down my text messages – there seemed to be hundreds of them – and the sweet condolences and goodbyes hammered home what I already knew, that life would never be the same. Among the voicemails was the message from Jack Straw saying he might be able to help and urging me not to quit. It had been left about 1 p.m. For a minute, I was overcome by a fresh wave of misery. Perhaps the justice secretary, trusted and respected by Gordon and Harriet, could have saved me? But there was no point thinking about it.

Mum came to collect me at the station, doing her best to be strong for me. She told me Sarah Brown had phoned her and Vilma to say how sorry she was about what had happened.

At home almost the first thing I saw was myself on the news. There was a clip of me making a crap joke about Boris Johnson during a speech at party conference. 'It looks like he's going to have to put his career as a stand-up comic on hold,' the journalist commented sarcastically.

I felt sick. 'Please turn it off,' I whispered.

My brother Phil was staying with Mum at the time and around 11.30 p.m. we slipped out of the house for a drink at the local pub. While we were there, Tony phoned.

'Peter, I am so sorry. Are you okay?' he said. He sounded really concerned, and wanted to know if there was anything he could do to help. He promised to phone later in the week.

In the pub, I poured out my heart to Phil, who seemed to be rather enjoying it all. I don't think he'd been involved in anything as exciting in his life. In the days that followed he became obsessed with the story, constantly checking the internet, TV and radio for updates. He loved the fact that he was involved in a national drama, and revelled in his role as counsellor to the chief protagonist.

Back in London, our neighbours were being brilliant. They'd rescued our dog Leo, who had been left in the house when Vilma fled with the kids; they were looking after the chickens; and they were sending us regular updates on the media scrum outside our home. When Vilma ventured back to London several days later, it was to the neighbours' place, from where she kept a wary eye on who was parked outside our property before deciding whether we could all come home.

En route to Waterloo the next morning, I looked down the train and saw my own face on the front of newspapers all along the carriage. I was getting weird looks and knew I was now being recognised. Philip Gould phoned, full of sympathy, and told me he was planning to defend me on Radio 4's *The World at One*. 'Someone's got to,' he said angrily.

Absurdly, the official party line was still that I was the only one who knew about the link between David Abrahams and the individuals who had made donations to the party. I knew this was unsustainable and would only fuel the scandal when journalists worked out who else had been involved.

Greg and I drafted my statement and headed over to the Electoral Commission's offices. By chance, we hailed what was probably the only taxi in London playing Gordon's monthly press conference on the radio. Predictably, the Prime Minister was being given a battering. He was not even attempting to defend what had happened, which was probably not surprising, since he hadn't gone to the trouble of finding out the facts. Far worse, he seemed to have turned into a legal expert. 'The money was not lawfully declared so it will be returned,' he pronounced.

Greg and I listened in dismay. 'That's just great. With friends like that...!' Greg quipped, trying to make light of it.

'Ha bloody ha,' I thought to myself. 'The Prime Minister has just publicly called me a criminal. Why doesn't he just ring the Met himself?'

My phone buzzed, the EC's number flashing up on the screen. I pressed 'reject' and waited for them to leave a message. It turned out they didn't want to see us. I suspected they were discussing whether to call in the police following Gordon's comments.

'Let's go anyway,' Greg said, so we pretended we hadn't received the message.

When we arrived, they seemed embarrassed to see us, so we thrust my statement at an official, and left.

'This might take a couple of months to sort out,' Greg said thoughtfully, as we snatched a sandwich afterwards.

It was a shock. Naively, I had imagined it would all be over in days. In between panicking about going to prison, I'd even had visions of being reinstated that very week. I remember desperately wanting to ask Greg whether I could go to jail, but I couldn't bring myself to voice this darkest of fears.

Back at Mum's everyone was trying to act normally, but I had experienced what I believe was my first panic attack. On the train home, my ears had started buzzing with a strange static noise, like the fuzzy crackling of a radio with a mobile phone too close. Hyperventilating,

I had removed the battery from my BlackBerry, hoping the knowledge that it could not ring would silence the strange buzzing in my head. It didn't work. The following day, I bought a new phone, telling only a handful of my closest friends and family the number. Filling out the contract, I did not know what to enter in the box marked 'occupation'. Was I now officially unemployed?

That night, and in the days that followed, Vilma was a fortress, but I could only sustain normality for an hour or so at a time. Then the constant churning in my stomach would get too much and I would have to get out of the house. At one point I disappeared for two hours, walking several miles in an attempt to clear my head. At home they were all panicking, and could not hide their relief when I returned in one piece.

On Wednesday, for the sake of something to do, Phil, Mum and I went to my sister Berni's house in Morden for lunch with her and Damien.

'Have you heard the latest?' Damien asked, as we walked through the door.

I didn't want to know, but it was a small house, and I could hear the TV bulletin from the front room. Gordon was being quoted condemning me in the Commons, and commentators were speculating on my fate.

My brothers started making prison jokes. They thought it was hilarious, but to me it felt all too real. I stumbled out of the house and leaned against the car, trying to breathe. 'Calm down. You'll get through this,' I told myself, though I wasn't sure I believed it.

At the pub with Phil that night, the landlady told us one of the regulars had recognised me and got very excited. 'He was going to call the papers. I said "Don't you dare!" and threw him out,' she said. I was grateful that there were people looking out for me.

By Thursday Vilma decided she'd had enough of hiding and was going home. I begged her not to, knowing there would still be journalists camped outside our house, but I knew she could not stay away much longer, not least because we had a number of foster children who had appointments that had been hastily rearranged.

Our role as foster parents made the crisis so much more difficult and frightening. We had kept social services informed from the start, but it was not a great career move having reporters staked outside the house, and though our supervising social worker was very supportive, we were scared about having the kids removed. Of particular concern was Ruby, the six-month-old baby we were caring for, who had massively bonded with us and was very settled. We had fallen in love with this little girl and were beginning to think about applying to adopt her. It was one of my worst fears that I might lose her.

There was some small consolation to finding myself out of work: I was finally able to spent some time with my children. On Wednesday night, for the first time ever, I attended Ben's school prize-giving ceremony. It was a very special moment for both of us, but the experience was marred by the sidelong looks I was getting from other parents. I knew they recognised me and were thinking I was dodgy.

On Thursday morning Vilma set off for London, having agreed to case the joint before entering the property. As she approached our street, she parked the car around the corner and walked to the neighbours' for coffee. While she was there, a journalist rang the doorbell.

'Hello, I was just wondering if you know the Watts next door,' the reporter said.

'Sorry, I'd better not talk about it,' Vilma replied sweetly, but it was enough to convince her not to stick around for long.

By now the party's claim that I was the only one who knew about the donations was unravelling and Jon Mendelsohn had admitted to being in the loop. He was under siege from the media and rang me in solidarity. My siblings were starting to get calls from the press and I was not particularly surprised when on Friday a reporter telephoned Mum. The net was closing and Poole no longer felt like a sanctuary.

In desperation, we arranged to move on: this time to my brother-in-law's flat in Tooting. Phil drove to London to drop me off and we went for a quick drink before he headed back to Mum's. We sat in a corner nursing our pints.

Suddenly, Phil leaned towards me. 'That bloke's giving you really funny looks,' he said, rolling his eyes towards a shifty-looking character a few tables away. The man got up and walked out of the pub, and my brother, enjoying himself hugely, hot-footed it after him at a discreet distance. Seconds later, he burst back in.

'He's phoning the bloody papers!' he hissed.

So we left immediately. I knew Phil wasn't winding me up because he would never willingly abandon a drink.

On Saturday night Cherie rang, and we spoke for what must have been almost an hour. She was very kind and kept asking if I needed anything. 'We've spoken to other people who want to help,' she said. 'If you need to speak to Alastair [Campbell] or David [Hill], just ring them,' she urged.

It was good to hear from her, and I felt a little less isolated. She must have gone to some effort to track down my new number. I took her advice and rang Alastair, David and Hilary Coffman, one of Tony's former press aides, and asked what they thought I should do about our foster kids. I was terrified about any of them being approached by the media, which I thought might tip social services over the edge, so Hilary put me in touch with someone senior from the Press Complaints Commission, who was very reassuring and gave me his mobile number in case anything happened.

I had arranged to see Greg in his office on Sunday to prepare a statement for the police interview. By now the Lib Dem MP Vince Cable had officially asked the Met to investigate, and I knew it was only a matter of time before I heard from them.

On the way to Greg's office, Paul Kenny, the general secretary of the GMB union, rang. 'I can't believe the way Gordon's treated you. I am so angry and I'm going to bloody tell him. It's a disgrace,' he said. He reminded me that I was a member of his union and that he would do anything he could to help. I was hugely grateful for this call, needing all the friends I could get.

Two weeks after my resignation the media frenzy finally began to die down. We decided to go home, and in the weeks that followed life began to settle into a new routine. While I was still obsessing about my situation, and had Google Alerts set up for 'Abrahams', 'donorgate', 'Watt' and just about every conceivable combination of all three, life was no longer entirely joyless. I was spending increasing amounts of time looking after Ruby, gradually taking over from Vilma as her primary carer. After years of tension over my job, which had left no room for quality time together, Vilma and I rediscovered that we actually quite liked each other.

However, I was struggling with being a nobody. I could not believe how status conscious I had become. Anxious to keep me busy, Vilma would issue me with lists of domestic tasks, and I became like Santa's little helper. In a funny sort of way I liked it, but it was a huge comedown from my former life. It was not easy to adapt to being so completely unimportant. I tried not to be ungrateful for Vilma's tolerance of the situation I had landed us in but it was difficult to hide my boredom.

I bitterly resented that the crisis had cast such a dark shadow over Vilma's pregnancy, which we had worked so hard to achieve through IVF. It was to be our first child together, and we were not able to enjoy it as we had hoped. There were times I was afraid that the stress of the scandal would put our unborn baby at risk.

I had also lost friends. Though the old gang – Marianna, Roy, Alicia and Hilary – were steadfast friends, and others in the party, Mike Griffiths, Margaret McDonagh and Tom Watson in particular, went out of their way to keep in touch, many more cut me adrift. An internal investigation was underway at HQ, and former colleagues were now afraid to talk to me. I did not blame them: by all accounts it was a witch hunt, such was the panic in Labour's high command. Staff were being issued with dire warnings to 'tell the truth or face the consequences'. I remember going for a drink with the old gang a few weeks after I quit, and they did not want to meet at our usual place because they were nervous about being seen with me.

Around mid-December, the police contacted me to say that they would interview me in Greg's office in the New Year. I was disappointed that it wasn't happening sooner, convinced that if I could just explain what had happened it would all go away. The days passed and I fell into a routine of domestic chores, outings with the children and late-night drinking.

At Christmas, No. 10 sent flowers, but I knew they were also talking to the police, and it wasn't to rally to my defence. Later I discovered that an attempt had been made to falsify minutes of the brief meeting I attended in Victoria Street, with Dianne, Harriet, and other NEC officers before my resignation. The document misleadingly suggested that I had admitted wrongdoing. One of those who was present at the meeting saw the account, which was written retrospectively, and demanded that it was corrected before being sent to the police. It was clear No. 10 badly wanted me charged, since it would cement their politically expedient characterisation of me as a renegade.

Shortly before my police interview in January Greg was invited to see the folder of evidence the police had collected on the case. He was not allowed to make copies, but took detailed notes of the documents which he showed me later. I was relieved that the investigation was progressing.

The important day finally arrived. Though I am not superstitious, I was wearing a pair of cufflinks Dad had given me shortly before he died. It was the second time in my career at the Labour Party that I had been interviewed by the police under caution, an irony that was not lost on the officers.

'Gather you're getting quite experienced at this. Do you need us to explain the procedure, or do you know it all already?' one of the detectives joked.

I laughed, but there was nothing funny about it.

Greg had briefed me not to get carried away during the interview. 'You talk too much, Peter, and you talk like a politician. You have got to learn to say less when you are interviewed, and answer the questions you are given, not the ones you'd like to be asked,' he coached.

But I had so much to get off my chest and couldn't wait to get started. The first point was that I had shown due diligence in the reporting of our donations. As General Secretary, it was my responsibility to ensure that the party's report to the EC was accurate, and I had gone to great lengths to do so. A team of about twenty-five people at HQ was involved in some way or other to ensure we got it right.

Secondly, I explained that I had been relaxed about the donations because I had inherited a set of relationships that I assumed the two previous General Secretaries had considered above board and acceptable. Nothing had changed since then.

I barely paused for breath as I ploughed on, explaining that donors gave us money in dozens of different ways, many of them far from straightforward. Not being straightforward didn't make them illegal. I had no idea about the nature of the relationships between different donors, and no General Secretary could have been expected to know such detail. Our systems ensured that all of the money came from legal donors (on an electoral register) and were all reported to the EC.

The police scribbled furiously, hardly able to get a word in. I had nodded obediently when Greg told me not to bombard them, but I was so outraged at the position I was in I could not hold back.

I explained that we knew that David had been giving money to his company directors and his solicitor and that an accountant had been involved. I said that as far as I was concerned they were the donors – they sent cheques and had been donors since 2003. I had no idea one of the individuals was a jobbing builder, and could not have been expected to know. As far as I was concerned, the involvement of an accountant and a solicitor was sufficient reassurance that all was above board.

The detectives shifted in their seats, occasionally glancing at their files. They had arrived with an interview plan, but I was battering them with so much information they didn't need it.

Greg wasn't stopping me, so on I went, telling them that the donations from David's associates constituted just 2 or 3 per cent of our total income. They were not that significant in the grand scheme of things, and I had no reason to pay them extra attention. Though I didn't tell the police, it is a mark of how relaxed the party was about the arrangements David had made that our fundraising division was trying to set up a similar structure involving a different donor, around the time of the 'donorgate' affair. I don't know who the donor was, but I know that Gerald was involved in exploring whether it would be above board and compliant with the rules.

After about four hours, the police said they had all they needed, and we wrapped up.

'You are the worst criminal I have ever represented,' Greg joked afterwards. 'I told you only to answer the question you are asked.'

He was laughing, and I knew he was pleased with my performance. He told me I had done very well, and I felt confident it was more than a lawyerly pat on the back. To be honest, I think we both thought that would be that. I went home feeling relieved, certain that the nightmare would soon end.

Yet weeks, then months, went by with no word from the police about the case. I would get the occasional call from No. 10, asking for updates, but there was never anything to report. However, I did warn them that if it ended in a trial, I would call Gordon, Harriet, Sarah Brown and others as witnesses. They would have to explain why, if I had done something so heinous in their opinion, I had been given repeated assurances that I would be looked after.

By February, after two months of unemployment, I was desperate to work. However, Vilma was about to give birth and we were starting to talk seriously about applying to adopt Ruby. She had been with us for just under a year, and we adored her and could not imagine giving her away. Having put my family second to my work for so long, I now wanted to prioritise them, and was lucky enough to find a position working for some friends who ran their own company and were both sympathetic and flexible enough to accommodate me.

In March, our daughter Gabriella was born, and for the first time since my resignation I stopped thinking about it. For a whole week, I floated about in an otherworldly state of paternal bliss. Gordon and Sarah sent us a quilted blanket with Gabriella's name embroidered on it. I'm ashamed to say my initial reaction was to use it as a dog blanket, but I knew I was just being childish and petulant. It was far too nice for that.

Later that month, I started in my new job full time. It was wonderful having money coming in again. Yet the case had not gone away. While there was radio silence from the police, officially I remained under investigation, which was not a helpful situation in relation to our adoption application for Ruby. Happily, social services were still supportive, and Greg wrote a very helpful letter explaining that this should be regarded as more of a civil than a criminal matter. He added that in the unlikely event that I was both charged and found guilty, the penalty would only be a fine. It was the first time I realised that whatever happened I was not going to prison. I remember thinking I should have just asked him about it before.

In early February 2009, fourteen months after my resignation, I discovered that the police had suddenly contacted the Labour Party asking for more information. I rang Greg.

'That doesn't sound very good, does it?' he replied worriedly.

Suddenly, the investigation felt very real again. I spent the next few weeks in agonised anticipation, terrified I was about to be charged, but still there was silence.

One spring Friday, when it seemed it would never end, I received a call from a journalist, asking if I'd heard the rumours that an announcement on my case was imminent. I hadn't, but the reporter called again on Monday to say the rumours were now very strong. Shortly after, Greg rang. 'I've had a call from the CPS saying they're going to make an announcement tomorrow,' he said.

'What does that mean?' I asked.

'Well, there are no certainties here, but I think it's going to be good news,' he replied.

He figured it would not make any sense for the CPS to announce they were about to charge me – if they wanted to charge me, it would make more sense to do so before publicising it.

I told Vilma, and it was as if I'd announced that the price of bread had gone up again. She barely reacted. It had been so long since the height of the drama that I think it had long stopped feeling real to her.

Someone from the Labour press office called, closely followed by a senior party official, and I told them that if I was cleared I would be making a statement. They were not at all keen, but there was nothing they could do.

'I'm angry about how I've been treated, and my statement will reflect that,' I warned.

The following morning, I went to Greg's office, as the CPS had promised to email him half an hour before making their announcement. We sat talking in his cluttered little room and continually pressing 'refresh' on his computer keyboard. Finally, the email we had been waiting for dropped into his inbox, confirming that there would be no charges.

'Congratulations. Quite right too,' Greg said, giving me a hug.

I rang Vilma and Mum, then got to work on my statement. My first draft was full of fury and I ripped it up. The second version was still way over the top, and I binned it too. By the third draft, I was becoming a bit more reasonable, but I didn't pull my punches.

'When this matter involving contributions to the Labour Party became a story I was abandoned by the political leadership of the Labour Party without regard for the impact this would have on me and my family.

'I was resolute then and now in my belief of my innocence and that I had acted in good faith. I wish the same good faith and loyalty had been shown to me,' I declared.

Meanwhile, a teleconference was underway between HQ and No. 10. 'Bad news,' one party official declared to another. 'Haven't you heard? They're not going to charge Peter. It would have been better for Gordon if he had been.'

To spare their blushes, I'll resist the temptation to divulge their names.

# 15. REFLECTIONS

So in the end, I was vindicated. On 7 May 2009, a full eighteen months after Gordon Brown unilaterally declared I had broken the law, the Crown Prosecution Service finally concluded what I had known in my heart all along: I had no case to answer.

The relief was immeasurable, but it was a pyrrhic victory. The episode had already cost me nearly everything.

I could fill a page with what I lost as a result of being the fall guy. But I know that however maligned I may feel, I have to take some responsibility for what happened. And I am proud that I took that responsibility. As General Secretary of the Labour Party, I always sought to lead from the front.

I believed and indeed still believe that David Abrahams was an honourable man who loved the party. However, I recognise that Labour's arrangements with him and his associates were ultimately wrong – not illegal, but certainly giving a sense of something not right. When it came to money, as a party we were always pushing the boundaries. I am sure that is still the case today. The truth is that fundraising for political parties is so difficult that those involved are frequently forced to stretch the law as far as it will go. The rule of thumb is that as long as the law is not actually broken, it is just about acceptable, though it can hardly be considered a very satisfactory system. It is one of the reasons I have been a long-standing supporter of state funding for political parties.

During 'cash for honours', a colleague was asked by the police whether they felt they had broken the spirit of the law. He replied that laws do not have spirits. In general I disagree. However, in the rarefied world of political fundraising, it was the letter of the law we focused on, or quite simply we would have gone bankrupt.

What is difficult to accept is that the Labour leadership knew this was the environment in which the fundraising division at HQ operated and they fully expected us to push the boundaries. Naively, I assumed that when things went wrong, it would therefore be treated as a team problem, rather than a problem for me alone. After all, it had been in the past.

As a result of a number of political scandals, public attitudes towards individuals who give large sums of money to political parties have become jaundiced. While it is right to be wary, it also seems right to start from the premise that donors are more likely to be altruistic than corrupt, given the levels of scrutiny they face. I can honestly say that none of the many wealthy donors I dealt with over the years ever indicated they expected anything material in return for their generosity. Luckily, there are individuals who are willing to donate to political parties because they truly believe in the work those parties are doing.

Naturally I have many regrets. My rise through the ranks of the Labour Party machine was perhaps too meteoric for my own good. I was just thirty-six when I became General Secretary, responsible for several hundred staff and earning a six-figure salary. My success went to my head and I began to feel invincible. I was complacent about my difficult relationship with Harriet, foolishly assuming I was powerful enough to do without her support. As soon as I was in trouble, I paid the price.

I regret ten years of lost opportunities with my older children: every parents' evening, sports day and prizegiving I missed. I kept putting my career first. The relationship I have had with my youngest children, Ruby and Gabriella, has been very different. I have been able to share their early years and now know just what I missed when I was too busy for their siblings. It is a shame that the police investigation overshadowed Vilma's pregnancy and our early days with Gabriella. There is a picture of me with our newborn when she was just a few minutes old. It was an amazing moment but as I cradled my daughter, wondering what life would hold for her, I remember suddenly thinking I might be prosecuted any day. I am sad that this special time was overshadowed.

I am also sad that I never had the chance to say goodbye and thank you to colleagues. I was hustled out without being able to tell them what a great job they do. Time and again they put themselves in the firing line for politicians, often for little or no recognition or gratitude.

I still feel terrible about the impact of the scandal on my mother, who was so proud of me and the job I did for the party. My resignation came just a few months after my father's death, when she couldn't have been more vulnerable.

Finally I regret that I spent so much time feeling sorry for myself. I should have been able to get over what happened more quickly. I allowed myself to wallow in misery. I suffered greatly, and on occasion I think I enjoyed the suffering quite a lot. Vilma now admits she was frightened at the state of me. I was not eating or sleeping, and I was drinking too much in the evenings. A few weeks after my resignation, I remember looking at myself in the mirror and barely recognising my reflection. I was on the verge of a breakdown but Vilma was fantastic, simply refusing to let me sink. Slowly but surely, she pulled me out of my self-pity, helping me re-establish some structure in my life. My recovery began when she encouraged me to start putting appointments into my empty diary – even if they were just to take the children swimming.

Perhaps what hurt most was the fact that following my departure, nobody publicly acknowledged my contribution to the party. It was as if my resignation, which was for the greater good of the party rather than because I was personally culpable, cancelled out the years of service. In the space of a week I went from a highly respected and popular head of the party machine to a leper. People I had protected when they themselves were in trouble queued up to attack me. It was a harsh lesson about the brutality of politics.

I am still proud of what I achieved. I grabbed the party's finances by the scruff of the neck, took the unpleasant decisions that were necessary to stave off the bailiffs and twice saved us from bankruptcy. I managed to keep the scale of the crisis quiet, so that only a handful of people knew just how close to the edge we came. I am proud of organising the transition of leaders and deputy leaders, which could have been bloody, but in the end wasn't. Though Tony probably left sooner than he would have liked, he went on his own terms. Finally, I am proud of the fact that I have survived. It was a horrendous two years, but my marriage held together, and our family grew.

Perhaps unsurprisingly, my view of politics has now changed. When I first joined the Labour Party, I was full of idealism. At the risk of sounding trite, what I cared about was making Britain a better place, by protecting the weakest and most vulnerable in society. Once I started working for the party, those lofty ideals were replaced by tribalism. It was all about winning: us versus them. Unfortunately, tribalism turns good men bad. They begin to lose their critical faculties, seeing everyone as either 'for' or 'against'. Some politicians and party officials enjoy tribalism more than the serious business of making the world a better place. At the height of my career, I was sometimes in danger of falling into this category.

That has changed. These days, when I hear Conservative politicians delivering speeches, I actually listen to what they are saying. Sometimes I even hear things I like. On balance, I still believe Labour offers the best solution to the country's ills – it's why I am still a party member. But I no longer believe we have all the answers. That may sound obvious to people outside the Westminster village, but after eleven years working for the party, I became institutionalised, losing my ability to judge positions and policies on merit.

My realisation that politics is not about good versus evil, but about finding the best solutions to the country's problems, no matter who has come up with the ideas, is partly the result of being outside the Westminster village for a while, and partly the result of the way I was treated. I finally realised we weren't always such good guys. I have had plenty of time since my resignation to rediscover the art of objectivity.

What about the people who knifed me? The truth is I am still angry with them. There are some individuals in politics who are weak and self-interested and allow those failings to overcome their purer objectives. For me, loyalty has always been everything, and I know that I would not have persecuted any colleague who was not indisputably, knowingly, and personally guilty of gross misconduct in the way that the Prime Minister and other senior figures persecuted me. My spectacular exit from the party was designed to take the heat off the leadership, but by erroneously declaring I had broken the law, then diving for cover, Gordon, Harriet and others simply succeeded in raising the stakes. The strategy was ill thought out and stupid, and I was manipulated. Labour has been rocked by many huge financial scandals, but I think I am the only person who was forced to resign accused by my own side for something I did not do.

It still amazes me that neither Gordon, nor Harriet, nor any other senior official in the party picked up the telephone to me when I was finally cleared by the Crown Prosecution Service. They did, however, find time to hold a teleconference at HQ in which regret was expressed that I would not be charged. When I discovered this conversation had taken place, it literally took my breath away. Perhaps Labour's high command would have felt less guilty about my departure if the police had agreed I had done something wrong? However, I suspect I am flattering myself that they gave it that much thought. For them, the caravan had long since moved on. The only person who really cared any more was me.

I have struggled not to be bitter, knowing forgiveness would be both worthier and healthier, but it has been immensely difficult to overcome my sense of betrayal.

I am getting there.

I know it is now time for me to move on.

# INDEX OF NAMES

relations with Tony Blair 2, 79,
81, 115
transition to PM 7–8, 19, 31–6,
112, 139–62
Brown, Sarah, wife of Gordon
Brown 123, 158, 161, 164–5,
188, 196
Bruce, Luke, former head of policy,
Labour Party 43
Bryant, Chris, Labour MP 141
Bush, President George W. 140
Byers, Stephen, former Cabinet
minister 174

Cable, Vince, Lib Dem MP 192
Cameron, David, Conservative
leader since 2005 7, 81–2,
116–17, 143, 166, 174–5
Campbell, Alastair, former press
secretary, No. 10 180, 192
Campbell, Sir Menzies, Lib Dem
leader 2006–7 115–16
Carter, Matt, General Secretary
of the Labour Party 2004–5
10–15, 23, 32
loans to Labour Party 38–43,
83–4, 88–9
Clarke, Ken, Conservative MP 29
Clarke, Nita, in Tony Blair's
political office 13–15
Clwyd, Ann, Labour MP 140
Coffman, Hilary, former press aide
to Tony Blair 192
Cohen, Ronnie, Labour Party
donor 168

Collins, Ray, General Secretary of
the Labour Party since 2008
13–14, 16–22
Cook, Greg, head of political
strategy, Labour Party 80
Cook, Robin, Labour MP, died
2005 74
Cruddas, Jon, Labour MP 156–7

David, Wayne, Labour MP 143
Dixon, Geoff, Labour Party
organiser 24, 30
Dobson, Frank MP, former Cabinet
minister 73
Dopemu, Tunde, friend of Vilma
Watt 146
Doughty, Nigel, Labour Party
donor 168
Dromey, Jack, NEC treasurer and
deputy general secretary of
Unite 41, 46–50, 58, 65, 94,
106, 114, 173, 180–83

Elder, Lord (Murray), friend of
Gordon Brown 8–9, 105, 183
Evans, Sir Christopher, Labour
Party donor and lender 62,
112

Fisher, Lee, schoolfriend of PW 27

Gardner, Tony, friend of PW from
Poole Labour Party 29
Garrard, Sir David, Labour Party
donor and lender 44, 46